What Will Susan Say?

What Will Susan Say?

✦

A Parable of Corporate Leadership

Edward A. Meagher III
with
Allison M. Paoli

iUniverse, Inc.
New York Lincoln Shanghai

What Will Susan Say?
A Parable of Corporate Leadership

iUniverse books may be ordered through booksellers or by contacting:

iUniverse
2021 Pine Lake Road, Suite 100
Lincoln, NE 68512
www.iuniverse.com
1-800-Authors (1-800-288-4677)

Because of the dynamic nature of the Internet, any Web addresses or links contained in this book may have changed since publication and may no longer be valid.

The views expressed in this work are solely those of the author and do not necessarily reflect the views of the publisher, and the publisher hereby disclaims any responsibility for them.

ISBN: 978-0-595-47118-8 (pbk)
ISBN: 978-0-595-70965-6 (cloth)
ISBN: 978-0-595-91398-5 (ebk)

Printed in the United States of America

This book is dedicated to my family, my partners, my clients, and a lifetime of colleagues who inspire, challenge, and care for me and what I believe in.
E.A.M.

Contents

Acknowledgments

I would like you to know that my wife Linda, who has been by my side since 1966, is the most special and inspirational person I know. Without Linda's life-long support and encouragement, I may have been digging ponds today rather than teaching leadership to some of the world's top executives and high-performing teams.

My two precious daughters have become some my best friends, constructive critics, and special young women, whom I both admire and love.

I would also like to thank Linda and Nikk Adams, two partners in Woodstone who mandated that I begin to write down some of my stories and share them with the public.

My global corporate learning came from two magnificent corporations, ITT in the 1970s and with PepsiCo for 16 exciting years during the 1980s and 1990s. I have had the privilege of working with some brilliant, talented and dedicated people whose intellect I have admired and whose value I cherished.

As a sixty-year-old man in the year 2007, I am fortunate enough to say that I have had the richest of great friends, amazing clients, and dedicated coworkers. Those very special people in my life have taken my ideas, sharpened them, and made them better. They share in my beliefs about leadership, and the value of becoming significant to the people we teach and care for.

Allison Meagher Paoli, my oldest daughter and partner in Woodstone Consulting, has been the driver behind *What Will Susan Say?* from its inception. She has crafted language, pushed me to be accurate and timely, and encouraged me to use the format of an executive leadership fable.

Book I

1

A Word of Introduction

To the American mind, the corporate executive is not entirely mortal. He or she is, as a category of entrepreneur, touched with superhuman powers. The decisions they make affect the lives of hundreds, thousands, hundreds of thousands—even millions of people. By their design and command, the U.S. economy is organized, its awesome power channeled and harnessed, making possible the most efficient free enterprise system the world has ever known. Never in the vast sweep of human history has there been such a citizen, wielding as they do far more economic influence than kings and queens of centuries past, any czar, sheik, or any Roman Caesar. Even in the aftermath of recent corporate scandals, the executive is invested with an authority once reserved only for royalty.

But there is a simple, disquieting reality that the American public has yet to fully accept: the CEO, CFO, COO, the vice president of marketing, the chief of advertising, with his or her meager Blackberry, briefcase, telephone and computer, is human after all. As a matter of course, they fail. And when they fail, it tends to be spectacular.

Executives are people whose lives have been defined by success. It's what they've become accustomed to. They begin their careers as proven academic stars who are then hired away by the corporations offering the most compelling challenges. What sets them apart in their new professional environment is their ability to quickly master the company technology, adeptly navigate the corporate bureaucracy, manage and design matters great and small—all courtesy of a first-rate intellect. And so they ascend through the corporate food chain with a speed that astonishes everyone around them. And then, at some undetermined point during this journey to the heights of corporate responsibility, it is overwhelmingly likely that this stellar career will stall. It may even collapse. The foremost question on their mind is, "How did it come to this?"

The mystery vexes not only the executive but their bosses, their subordinates, company shareholders, the board of directors—and certainly their spouses. Their struggle becomes a quicksand metaphor, as the harder they work, the faster they sink. They find the mystery especially agonizing, as their analysis leads them to conclude that the root cause of their failure is one of aptitude and initiative. And yet they have simply been doing what has worked so well for them in the past—being the intellectual superstar, the smartest person in the room, and the hardest worker. But now the reliable old magic seems to have deserted them. It's as though at some undetermined moment they crossed an invisible threshold and passed into a realm where the old laws of corporate governance no longer apply.

The phenomenon is commonplace. Failure rate of newly promoted executives typically exceed 40% in the first eighteen months and comes at a cost to the company of two to five times the executive's annual salary. It often takes a far greater toll on company prestige. Some 68% of new businesses fail. Mergers and acquisitions have an even steeper wall to climb, with an attrition rate of 80%. But one should bear in mind that all such colossal business failures are the cumulative result of thousands of *individual* failures.

If the struggling executive's plight is typical, then so is its cause: an inability to navigate a new and complex business culture and political landscape that has been changing imperceptibly on their journey to the summit of corporate responsibility. It is this slow accretion of small changes that, over time, has ultimately changed everything.

As the executive was happily ascending through the ranks of American business, the importance of their technical expertise and cold intellectual capacity slowly receded. At the top all of that is taken for granted. In this rarified atmosphere, they are surrounded by technical brilliance and expertise; all of their peers are products of the same education, and possess an intellect capable of illuminating the most abstract realms. But while everyone was learning the basics of the company business and being promoted for their quick study, the ability to assemble and inspire effective teams became paramount. Nobody told them that, at the top of the corporate ladder, building strong teams is what the game is all about.

Incredibly, this most important and basic of executive skills is not taught in a college accounting courses or in any MBA program, nor is it imparted in the board room. As counter-intuitive as the concept is to the hyper-competitive corporate mind, it is also true: you help yourself at the office by helping those around you.

Top leaders have another ability in common. They are masters at understanding and managing their emotions, and this is what sets them apart from their brilliant but less successful peers. They know how to manage people and relationships, and effortlessly seem to inspire loyalty and commitment. It's this impalpable ability that allows them to unlock hidden strengths—not only in themselves but *in those around them*. Their success is derived from what we all know deep down: we need other people to succeed.

All of this sounds very simple, and if it were, I would be out of a job, and corporate America would be one big, happy, profitable community. Of course this isn't the case, particularly in a culture that so assiduously celebrates the self-sufficient pioneer, the rugged individual, the self-made millionaire. Teamwork is happy-face twaddle, for there is a little bit of Davey Crocket and John Wayne in us all, a default preference to go it alone, to succeed or fail on our own terms. As Steve Jobs famously called out, "It's better to be a pirate than join the Navy."

We Americans can't get enough of this independent, renegade spirit. But in a sense the mantra is so much empty rhetoric. We need to bear in mind that Jobs went on to form one of the most successful teams in the history of American enterprise, and it wasn't through a failed attempt at marshalling the efforts of a band of freelancing buccaneers. As capable, talented and motivated as the American executive typically is, attempting to form an effective team from a group of pirates, cowboys, cowgirls, or what have you, can be the single greatest challenge of their career. Until they can master this art, the next level of success will always remain just beyond their grasp.

2

The Corporate Animal

My career has taken me around the world more times than I care to remember. At age twenty-four I was negotiating communications industry agreements throughout the Western hemisphere, Europe, and Southeast Asia for ITT World Communications, Inc. Eight years later, I was recruited to PepsiCo, Inc., where I worked in labor relations, and became the first vice president of human resources for the PepsiCo Division (PFSI). In this capacity I was responsible for the development of new companies in more than forty countries that would go on to manufacture and sell PepsiCo products globally. My chief responsibilities were to develop a sound organizational design and to enhance the company's team effectiveness. More recently, I've been a consultant to the United States Nordic Combined Ski Team, providing coaching services to several Olympic teams. In June of 2000, the Woodstone Leadership Model, which I've been developing in one way or another throughout my career, was selected for use in the U.S. Nordic Combined Ski Team's performance effectiveness initiatives for the World Cup competition, and for the 2002 Winter Olympic Games in Salt Lake City.

This is to say that my experience is wide, and I've seen a few things. Most significantly, I've seen American big business at work in a variety of cultures, and I've seen how it operates from the bottom up, the top down, and from the inside out. What I've come away with is the understanding that, in general, we Americans are an open people who are not only willing but eager to talk about what bothers us, what motivates us, what we like and what we loathe. American corporate culture, however, breeds a different kind of animal, one that isn't altogether open to talking about intangible things such as how matters affect them emotionally, concepts such as teamwork, or the essence of great leadership. Forming great teams certainly is not our strong suit.

As a result, the American corporate creature often makes a poor teammate. Why? There are several reasons, foremost of which is that they are not as adept at developing effective relationships with their subordinates and peers as they should be. Nor are they adept at managing the complexities of guiding vast businesses run by human beings who are motivated, guided, inspired, thwarted and frustrated by their emotions. And worse yet, American corporate executives often share the bad habit of competing against one another rather than focusing their attention and energy on marketplace competitors. In order to harness their energies and ideas, the effective leader or team member has to be open to understanding the people they are surrounded by in their working world. They have to have some understanding of what peers think and feel. Perhaps more than any other, this latter character trait is what sets the successful executive apart from all the rest. Developing this kind sort of awareness is an aptitude, and like any aptitude, it can be learned.

Great leaders are made, not born, and with careful study they can be emulated. And this has been my chosen field of study. I have found that one of the best ways to understand the nature of great leadership is to dissect the anatomy of a particular career, to study the biographical arc of a professional life and see what makes it tick. The most vivid lessons come from those leaders who experience great success and then go on to fail when confronted by common human weaknesses in the ever-changing business environment. They excel in their careers, advancing to greater and greater heights, until their Achilles' heel is inevitably revealed to them.

These are the people I have learned the most from, and one stands out from all the rest. For me there has been no greater example than that of a friend and mentor of mine, and his remarkable story elucidates nearly every element of the Woodstone Model, which I have been cobbling together over the course of the last few decades. Seeing this drama unfold over the years was enormously instructive for me, for it reaffirmed what I've always known in my bones to be true: In the world of business, good relationships trump technical and creative brilliance. To my mind, his story is a living illustration of why talented people succeed, while other equally talented people fail.

I wrote this book because I know the secret to the success of companies like Starbucks and Wal-Mart. I also know why certain leaders of large corporations failed so spectacularly. It wasn't because of poor market conditions, a flawed strategic vision, or because these CEOs were famously too aggressive in their efforts to cut costs. They ran aground because they failed in their relationships with the people around them. This is what caused them to stumble as leaders, and this is why their companies either underperformed or were driven into the ground altogether.

This brings me to my final point. The reason a corporate leader, a manager, or even an ambitious business undergrad at some state university would want to buy and read this book is because it will help them understand how to succeed as leaders. Such a book has a persuasive argument grounded in real-life experience to back it up. In this book, my argument is advanced by way of a story—the story of a career that succeeds as a result of the protagonist's cultivation of his relationships. That career, however, comes off the tracks the moment those relationships begin to suffer, and the consequences are swift and severe not just for him, but for an entire company. I chose to make my case in the form of a parable, so that the reader would be able to comprehend more fully and viscerally the nature of my ideas. So I'll begin with this person who was once very close to me. His name is Steve.

3

Little Seeds

From afar his family appeared unremarkable.

He was born in the upper Bronx to a Catholic family in 1945. Dad was a police officer, Mom stayed home to raise him and his two little sisters. As an adolescent he demonstrated a natural aptitude for sports, but he was slight of build. His most obvious talent showed itself in the classroom. Early on in grammar school, this kid dazzled his teachers with his brilliant mathematical mind.

Steve's academic gift was enhanced by his father's insistence that the boy succeed in school. Although his dad was happy in his job, he didn't want this kind of career for his son. Day in and day out, his father came in contact with career criminals, domestic strife, and everyday urban squalor. This boy was made for greater things, which was evident with each unblemished report card he brought home. Steve's mother was less concerned with her son's academic performance; she insisted only that he have a sound moral compass. The worst thing he could do in life was to hurt or humiliate another person. So in Steve's formative years, his career was rooted in a fertile soil of love and discipline.

He could have gone to the college of his choosing after high school, but family finances were tight, and in the winter of 1963 Steve was awarded a full academic scholarship to NYU. The business curriculum there was good, and the accounting program exceptional. The only expenses he would incur were for room and board in Greenwich Village, which he could manage with a job as a janitor in a precinct arranged through a friend of his father.

During the next four years Steve quenched his academic thirst in the tiny garden-level apartment that he shared with two philosophy students. He immersed himself not only in his business and accounting course work, but in military history, chemistry, botany and zoology. Apart from his business and accounting courses, he liked his history classes. He studied the lives of great men who changed the world, reading biographies of Alexander the Great, Napoleon, Jefferson, and Churchill. But his business and accounting courses always dominated his time. One day while reading a business text at a local pub, his gaze fell upon a young woman with black hair and blue eyes. She was staring at him from where she sat at a window table, and, on a whim, Steve walked over and introduced himself. With a shy handshake she introduced herself as a sophomore art history student at NYU and religious studies. Her name was Susan.

What followed was a brief and intense courtship. Both were by nature studious, both Irish Catholic, both products of working-class families and New York public school educations. Steve noticed that his roommates and friends had a tendency to fall in love with her, possessing as she did that irresistible combination of street and academic smarts. She knew the Yankees lineup intimately, and she recognized the difference between Greek and Roman architecture. Why she seemed to have settled on Steve remained a mystery to the slightly built business and accounting major.

By Steve's junior year at NYU, the Vietnam War was heating up, and with it came all the wrenching social changes in New York City. As he and Susan came to know one another, they discovered that they shared a similar view of the chaotic world in which they found themselves. They were tantalized by the counterculture, finding it new and exciting, especially in the early years, but remained observers of what was going on all around them. Steve understood the underpinnings of the protests in the streets, and yet he wanted nothing more than to see the U.S. prevail in Southeast Asia. Once he took Susan to see Country Joe and the Fish at the Purple Onion where they sipped vodka and danced, while everyone around them took it a step or two further. So the young couple was drawn together. They were part of a generation that was in the midst of rebelling against their parents, but Steve and Susan wanted to emulate theirs.

At age twenty-one, Steve was first and foremost a student. So it was natural for him to become a student of Susan. This is how he would come to know her—by relentlessly quizzing her about her upbringing, her parents and family. One day she mentioned to Steve that her brother had recently entered the priesthood. Then she dropped a bombshell. She herself, she said, had once given serious consideration to becoming a nun.

"I'm glad I didn't go through with it," she said, "but I wanted you to know because it's a part of who I am."

Instead of a convent, she'd decided upon NYU where she had immersed herself in religious studies—a lonely field in the late 1960s. She was the first woman in her family to go to college, and she loved everything about her new life. She loved her elective drama classes, she loved the city. "And now," she said, "I'm in love with a business and accounting major." A little later in the conversation she confessed that she was now coming around to seeing herself as a mother rather than as a nun.

When Steve thought about it, he realized that he should not have been surprised that Susan had considered becoming a nun. There was something ethereal about her. This mystical air seemed to be a family trait, an aspect Steve found deeply fascinating. One evening, while they watched the ships chugging up and down the Hudson River from Battery Park, Steve asked Susan to marry him.

4

Irwin

They were married the day after graduation, whereupon Steve enrolled in Columbia's MBA program. Meanwhile, Susan took a position as an art teacher at a Lower Eastside public elementary school, and together they set up house in small second-floor apartment three blocks away. To make ends meet, Steve took a job offered by Arthur Andersen that paid his tuition and offered a small sign-on bonus. The work was academic for Steve, and allowed the newlyweds a comfortable, uncluttered life together. Soon Arthur Andersen offered a more lucrative job as an auditor, which gave them a small savings account and provided for a modest summer vacation. More significantly, it allowed them to entertain thoughts of children. They were happy as either of them had ever been, and there was a developing sense that it was only going to get better.

Steve's academic life was also coming alive. He was about to make a friend who would shape his professional life in ways he could never have imagined.

During his second semester at Columbia, Steve met a fellow MBA student by the name of George Irwin in his corporate strategy class. Everyone called him Irwin, and he was extraordinary by any measure. Day-in and day-out, he asked the most brilliant questions Steve had ever heard a student put to a professor. The queries involved accepted approaches to branding and corporate marketing. But he also asked specific questions about how creative teams worked, why they were structured the way they were, why they tended to be so large and seemingly unwieldy. The faculty loved him. From Steve's point of view, it appeared as though Irwin was grooming himself for an extraordinary career. Irwin was so intriguing to Steve that he asked him to have a beer at the student union one Friday afternoon. It was here, among a throng of students, that Steve asked Irwin about his background.

"Graduated from Brown last year," he said, speaking just as rapidly as he did in class. "I just don't understand how corporations develop great ideas through these huge committees. Wouldn't you rather have individuals working by themselves, or maybe have small teams developing concepts?"

Steve could only shrug.

"Tell me what you think?"

"I don't know enough to offer an opinion," Steve said. "So you're going to go into advertising after this?"

"Marketing and advertising," Irwin said. "You're a local boy, I'll bet."

"The Bronx. And you?"

"Upper East side."

Then he and Steve shook hands. The exchange had been the first thirty seconds of what would be a very long and intense relationship. But neither of them could have guessed where it would eventually lead.

◆   ◆   ◆

From the beginning the two friends recognized that they complemented one another in a very specific way. Irwin had far-flung ideas that encompassed everything from new businesses he wanted to develop, to new products he wanted to patent, to new techniques he wanted to employ in order to market them. Steve, on the other hand, could look at numbers and see patterns. For him the numbers told a story. To Irwin's amazement, Steve could look at five years of a company's balance sheets and read them like a narrative: "... here the company began to struggle even though interest rates were holding steady ... but their energy costs spiked at the same time, and began cutting into the margins ... which led to the layoffs the following quarter, but by then it was too late ..."

One was creative, the other analytical. Should the time ever come when they worked together, they thought they would be unstoppable.

Steve found Irwin the single most intriguing person his own age that he'd ever met. One thing struck Steve as odd, however. Irwin always seemed reluctant to share details of his family or upbringing. Whenever the subjects came up, Irwin's voice grew quiet. It happened every time. Whenever Steve couldn't get a word in edgewise with Irwin, he would say something like, "You know, I've never met your parents," Irwin's voice would instantly fall silent, and Steve could say what he wanted.

Over the course of the next two years, Steve learned little more than the following: his friend had two younger brothers, and it had been up to Irwin to oversee their welfare when they were growing up. Both parents held high-powered positions as stock analysts at Merrill-Lynch, and rarely spent time with the kids when they came home from school. Taking care of his two little brothers had been Irwin's job as an adolescent. During his undergraduate years at Brown he had tutored high school kids in Providence in order to make a little extra money, even though his parents were very well off. He'd never had a free ride. Like Steve, Irwin had a strong academic bent, and had even given serious thought to becoming a business professor. During his MBA work at Columbia, however, he'd gotten the urge to dive into the corporate world, an interest acquired from his parents.

One weekend Irwin took Steve and Susan out to his parents' house just outside of East Hampton. A pebble driveway meandered under a canopy of oak trees to a small mansion with four huge pillars standing before the front door. The house was set atop a bank of sand dunes, with a boardwalk wandering from the back deck all the way down to the Atlantic Ocean. The interior was nearly as astonishing. Tucked away here and there in the house were little knickknacks and landscape paintings and drawings by well known regional artists whom Susan recognized. The house was sprawling. Steve could scarcely imagine that a single family could have accumulated so much wealth, but he was quickly becoming comfortable with the idea.

Saturday afternoon Irwin's girlfriend Sheila came by. She was a curator at a small Manhattan museum with short jet-black hair and wide brown eyes. She and Susan not only looked alike, they shared interests in everything from art history to motherhood. Within the first few minutes of meeting, it seemed they'd been friends forever. During the daytime the two young couples relaxed among the sand dunes and swam in the sea, and at night the women had a glass of Mateus, while Steve and Irwin broke out a twelve-year-old bottle of J&B scotch. Just as the sun was setting on their last night together, Irwin took Sheila's hand and stood up.

"This time next year," he said as though making an announcement, "we'll be two old married couples."

"Irwin wanted you two to be the first to know," Sheila said, as she held out her hand to show off her engagement ring.

Steve reached for Susan's hand. He then stood and proposed a toast: "To the brilliant and beautiful Irwins."

Their glasses chimed. As they sipped their cocktails and the crescent moon rose over the Atlantic, the four of them knew they were in the company of friends they would have for the rest of their lives.

5

$60,000

Steve's performance as an auditor at a Big-Eight accounting firm was all it took to launch what would become an amazing career. At age twenty-five he was recognized by his supervisor as a remarkable talent; however, what set him apart was harder to quantify. He was brilliant with numbers, but so were all the accountants the firm hired. What Steve possessed was the perfect disposition for working closely with big, conglomerate clients. When people did not like a particular audit, or disagreed with the larger picture that Steve's numbers painted, he calmly clarified himself, explaining step-by-step how he had arrived at a particular conclusion. Most significantly, he was never arrogant, and took the time to make himself clear. Even Arthur Andersen's client companies came to love him.

One of these client companies was PMG Global Communications. PMG became so fond of Steve that they offered him a job prior to his graduation from the Columbia MBA program. Steve accepted it on the spot. It was a job handmade for a brilliant grad student of limited means, for they paid his tuition and a salary three times what he had been making at Arthur Andersen. Steve logged twenty hours per week at the office while the rest of his time was devoted to his MBA course work, and to Susan.

The young couple's lives were busy but tidy. Upon graduation Steve went to work fulltime for PMG and was put in charge of a team of fifteen auditors. At age twenty-eight he found himself flying around the world, reviewing the auditing functions of companies on three different continents. The only significant downside was the extended travel, which left Susan home alone for a third of every month. But that wouldn't last.

Over dinner one night in their tiny apartment she announced to Steve that he was going to be a father. Steve proposed that they leave immediately for a bed-and-breakfast in New Hampshire to celebrate. Susan, however, pointed out that they both had to work. In the place of a romantic vacation, Susan tried to figure out their finances, while Steve was off on a KLM flight to Brussels to review the work of his team auditing a conglomerate of sister European radio stations.

Over the course of the first trimester, Susan prepared a corner of their bedroom for the coming baby. Meanwhile Steve's career found its footing. Impending fatherhood turned him into something of a coach with his team of auditors, especially when they were working in one of those parts of the world where corruption was a standard practice. Whenever the team was confronted with altered books or deliberately obscure accounting, Steve had his people stop cold in their tracks in order to get to the root of the problem. In one instance in the Windward Islands of the Caribbean, his lead accountant was expected to pay a $60,000 bribe to the customs officials. Without it, PMG would be unable to bring their collateral into the country, and PMG's business there would be effectively crippled until the bribe was paid. When Steve refused to authorize the payment, he suddenly found himself in a swamp of local political intrigue.

From a strict business standpoint, paying the $60,000 bribe made sense, as it would facilitate more than $15 million in business over the next year. Thus, when Steve refused to authorize the payment and ordered a halt to all work, it caused the PMG people in the field to panic.

"We're not in Kansas anymore," the accountant explained. "Bribery isn't corruption here. It's business as usual."

"Doesn't matter," Steve replied. "We can't do it."

Steve did not completely comprehend the magnitude of his problem, and a few of his colleagues quietly began to accuse him of being grossly naive, of having, as one of them put it, "jug-handle ears." Others claimed the twenty-eight-year-old was making an annoying display of piety for his audience at the New York office, and was holding up the transaction of millions of dollars of business in the process. Somebody needed to explain to the pencil neck how things worked in the world of international business.

Even Steve began to suspect that he was being too unyielding for the job. Somewhere deep in the back of his mind he understood the bribery conflict to be the accountant's equivalent of the gutter life his father had endured and had always felt tainted by as a New York City cop. And now, as a head auditor, he saw himself in the role of a financial police officer. And who knew? Maybe he would pay the $60,000 after all. Maybe he would turn out to be a corrupt financial cop, someone his father would arrest for malfeasance. But in the furthest reaches of his mind, Steve wanted the purity of Susan's brother's life, not the grit of his father's.

In any event, his dilemma was real, and to his mind he was being practical, not pious. His refusal to authorize the bribe stemmed from the fact that he would be the one who would have to sign off on the misappropriated $60,000. His signature would be attached to it—*forever*. He understood that his company's standards and the standards of certain countries were not one and the same. Moreover, he knew that his board of directors understood this. And yet he also knew that, over time, this kind of systemic corruption put him and his auditors in an untenable professional and legal position, and he simply did not want to begin his career in this fundamentally compromised way, even if the bribe had the tacit blessing of the company's chief financial officer. It wasn't some technical legal jeopardy he could find himself in. He saw himself as being responsible for the shareholders' money, and he took that responsibility very seriously. That was the very core of his job.

6

The Analyst

Immediately upon his return to New York, Steve requested a transfer within the company to a position that was essentially analytical and strategic in nature. It was a stand-alone, ivory tower post that offered little contact with anyone but the V.P. overseeing his work. What it did require was a brilliant mind that could penetrate complex strategy and marketplace dynamics. It also demanded that the person take in a flurry of new proposals and assess the inherent risks. He or she had to be able to see—through a veil of numbers—what no one else could see. What it required was a powerful mind capable of taking in vast spreadsheets from which that person could paint a picture of the future.

Clearly, the job was a more comfortable fit for Steve. At least in the beginning. He was tired of ten-hour plane flights, and tired of being away from Susan for three or four days every week. With the baby coming in five months time, he wanted to be closer to home as a matter of routine.

If some thought Steve was a bit too sweet, his bosses recognized that he was also gifted. Steve didn't report his opinions. He was known to report what he *saw*, and his boss interpreted the $60,000 bribery matter as evidence of this. His reports were irrefutable, and, as a result, he was granted his strategy job where his conscience could remain clean and his reputation unsullied.

Although the new job was isolating, Steve was doing what he enjoyed and what he was good at, and was being paid handsomely to do it. Moreover, the VP he reported to took his opinions seriously. Although the VP was exceedingly cool and aloof, Steve had few complaints. His life seemed to be expanding in extraordinary and unexpected ways. That fall, Susan gave birth to a seven-pound baby girl whom they named Sarah, and suddenly they were part of a family of their own making.

The new job fit his new life. Steve had to travel to the PMG's London office, but only on occasion. At the New York office he would meet with the general manager and CFO, and together they would carry out a thorough review of the financial reports and the company books. But the job slowly became mundane. After three months into his tenure, he decided to go out on a limb and back a new satellite communications technology. PMG, he was sure, could benefit in a number of important ways. As Steve saw it, new markets would be made available to their radio stations, and they would become far more competitive in those markets which they were already in.

What his proposal required was a $2.2 million capital investment (a lot of money at the time) in what was widely thought to be an unproven technology. This gave the proposal real downside risk. If the satellite was successfully launched but the technology didn't work, the project would be a complete loss, as it would literally be beyond anyone's reach to fix the problem. If the rocket exploded on the pad, then it would all be a very expensive fireworks show.

Few of Steve's colleagues saw the whole picture—the one Steve saw. The markets would only be marginally improved and expanded, they argued, and the risk of the technology failing to come online was huge. Steve, however, had researched both of these concerns exhaustively, and had learned that this new technology was far more reliable than what had come before it. The chief difference was a failsafe backup that all but ensured the system would work once safely in orbit. Steve was adamant, and claimed the capital outlay would pay for itself in eighteen months. Several colleagues argued that it would take seven to ten years to see a return—*if* everything went precisely according to plan. As he and Susan went to bed one evening, the phone rang. To his surprise, it was his VP informing him that he was lending his support to Steve's proposal.

"I think it could take the company to the next level," the VP said.

"If we don't do this, our competitors will," was Steve's response.

Two days later PMG's CEO gave the go-ahead for the project as well, and Steve knew his job was on the line. The following October the satellite was launched. There were no explosions on the launch pad, no overwhelming solar storms to fry the electronics. When the technical team flipped the last switch to bring the satellite online, the panel instantly came alive.

As the results came in over the course of the next year, they were even better than Steve had predicted. PMG was now able to send media content around the globe at minimal cost and at a moment's notice. The content was more varied and improved, and PMG's affiliates were thrilled. Overnight they were competitive in markets that had previously languished. At age thirty, Steve suddenly had a reputation in the industry as a prophet. He wasn't a "strategic thinker" but a wizard with a crystal ball.

7

Good Press

The story made the business pages of every metropolitan newspaper in America, and was given plenty of ink by the *Wall Street Journal*. As a result, an executive search firm with international reach quietly went about researching the people who had foreseen PMG's potential in the realm of satellite communications. This was the Coulter Group. One of the names that came to their attention was that of Steve's VP. He was widely recognized as "brilliant," having established a solid reputation for success that stretched back nearly twenty years. But he also had a solid reputation for arrogance. The Coulter Group wanted the brilliant mind without the corrosive personality that they, as top-drawer corporate headhunters, were all too familiar with. Another name that came to their attention was Steve's. The subordinate, they slowly came to realize, was the satellite project's parent. He was also more in line with the kind of executive they usually targeted.

Jeffery Everett, a 36-year-old partner of the Coulter Group, had been tasked by a large conglomerate client with finding a handful of up-and-coming execs to lead a number of their small, recently acquired companies. The client just happened to be PMG's chief rival, TTM, and they had grown alarmed with the lack of great candidates the Coulter Group, or any other search firm, had produced. Everett himself had become so frustrated that he'd even considered dropping the assignment altogether, as each of these particular GM positions would require someone with two key personality traits that they rarely found in one person. They had to be analytical in nature, Everett believed, and they had to be natural collaborators.

◆   ◆   ◆

One evening after work, while Steve and Susan were doing the dishes, the telephone rang.

Jeffery Everett introduced himself, and began going on and on about Steve's graduate work at Columbia, his work at Arthur Andersen, and his tenure at PMG. Everett was impressed by the call Steve had made with PMG's communication satellite, but far more impressed with how he had handled his auditing work, particularly when he was leading the team of auditors for Arthur Andersen.

"Our clients are truly blown away by that kind of leadership," he said. He then asked Steve if he had time to meet later that week.

"I could squeeze in a few minutes," Steve said.

Steve was flattered. Privately, however, he was certain nothing would come of the meeting. He was content where he was, doing what he was doing in his tiny Lower Manhattan office. But as promised, Steve left work a few minutes early on the appointed day, and then dropped by for the meeting. After a casual conversation, Everett asked, "Have you ever thought about running a company?"

"Not seriously," Steve said.

"I bet you'd be great at it."

Everett then moved on to other subjects, and before Steve knew it, Everett was asking him if they could meet again in a few days' time.

"I'm happy at my present post," Steve said.

"As a strategist?" Everett said as though surprised.

Steve nodded. His enthusiasm for his present job was less than obvious.

"In my opinion," Everett went on, "running your own company is the greatest challenge in all of business."

Steve's eyes widened. Talk of great challenges was like catnip to Steve, and he suspected that this was why Everett had brought up the subject. Everett, Steve noticed, concluded the meeting, saying, "There's nothing like running your own show."

During their meeting the following week Everett convinced Steve to discuss "opportunities" with his clients. Again, Steve agreed, and later that afternoon he found himself in a boardroom surrounded by TTM people. They kept the topics general as they asked Steve about his long-term plans. Those plans, he replied in so many words, were to continue doing what he was doing.

Once Steve had left, the TTM people could hardly contain their enthusiasm. Here was the real thing. Eventually one of the analysts tossed out the possibility of having Steve take on their biggest challenge. It was something completely different from the strategic work he was doing, but would offer Steve an enormous incentive if he succeeded.

The idea was to recruit him to run the Gunther Company, a failing sprinkler/fire suppression manufacturer TTM had recently acquired. Steve, they all agreed, had the temperament and certainly the intellect. At this point, Everett stood up to make a point.

"A company as complicated as Gunther needs a particular kind of chief," he said.

"Smart and tough," the TTM analyst suggested.

"More smart and less tough," Everett replied. "You've got people from every walk of life working for you, and if the boss manhandles them, they're going to drop him on a dime."

"It's a tough place, Everett," a colleague countered. "A touchy-feely soul will get chewed up and spit out."

"The employees aren't that tough," Everett said. "You've got to have some-body in there with the ability to step outside of himself and see the world from someone else's point of view."

"You like this guy."

"I have to tell you," Everett said as he slowly drummed his fingers on the tabletop. "He impresses me. His father's a retired cop, but he's not taken with his own authority. Everybody who's ever worked for him loves him. He's got a spine, which he has demonstrated in the past, and he's obviously smart. He's *completely* humble … I'm telling you, guys like him can transform entire companies."

◆   ◆   ◆

The Long Island-based Gunther Company designed, manufactured, sold and installed sprinklers in high rise buildings. Its average annual growth over the past several years had been an anemic 1.4%, while inflation had been many times that. And now TTM was looking for someone who could make it grow at an annual rate closer to 15% to 16%.

But no one, including Everett, really thought that Steve would give up what he had to take such a job. He was a strategic planner with a single direct report. The Gunther Company was old school. It was manufacturing. It was messy. It had no glamour. When they approached Steve with the idea at their next meet-ing, however, everyone was taken aback.

"That's a very interesting idea," Steve said. "Very, very interesting."

But Steve in fact had serious reservations, and as he drove home from the meeting, he considered each and every one of them.

Were Steve to take such a job, he would be stepping down from his ivory tower. The Gunther Company was a world of hard-and-fast responsibility. As a planner he had been advising others. As a GM, he would be receiving, rejecting or accepting advice. He would be responsible for a company of just over three-hundred employees. He would hold their jobs in his hands. He would be responsible for the shareholders' investment. As appealing as running a company sounded, Steve knew that Everett was right: there was no greater challenge in all of business. And he was up for it.

8

An Enduring Friendship

Steve and Irwin had managed to keep in regular touch over the years even though their careers now dominated their lives. Irwin was currently working with a monumentally successful boutique advertising firm, and stunning the industry with his genius and energy. His smart and funny campaigns were credited with having breathed life into dying companies that had formerly been written off by Wall Street. The stock price, which reflected the investment community's conventional wisdom, would be in the tank. And then, just as the company was about to dissolve in a pool of red ink, Irwin would be invited in to pull a rabbit out of his hat in the form of a television campaign that captured the imagination of the entire nation.

In recent years, Steve and Susan had taken unbridled pride in watching the television commercials dreamt up by their good friend. Now he was recognized as a force of nature in the advertising world, and whenever Steve had to make a major business decision, he always called Irwin. Steve valued no one's business perspective more.

"You'll be great at it," was Irwin's first reaction to the news of Steve's job offer.

"It's a manufacturing plant."

"I understand," Irwin said. "But you have a knack for coming off as caring for people—because you actually do. People sense that. When D-Day rolls around, you're storming Omaha Beach with an army behind you."

"This isn't a John Wayne movie," Steve said. "It's running a light manufacturing plant on Long Island."

"Trust me," Irwin said. "You know how to talk to blue collar and white collar guys over lunch. Drop the planning job. You were born to lead."

Although he was now older, Steve was still a shy personality who never truly thought of himself as a leader. He knew that he could work with what the headhunter called "the full spectrum of the workforce"—from the mailroom jockey in the basement to the CEO in the corner office. But Steve saw this capacity as only one component of leadership. There was something more to what it meant to gain the trust of people to the extent that they would follow you through the jungle of the workaday world.

During his next meeting with the TTM people, Steve was taken out to the Gunther plant which lay midway out on Long Island. The three-acre building sat on an eight-acre property, and was surrounded on three sides by parking lots and recently planted white maple saplings. The building was abuzz with activity when they came through the foyer and stepped onto the polished concrete floor. Welding stations were staggered along an assembly line where men in welding helmets fastened fittings to pipes beneath rows of hanging florescent lamps that threw off a dismal yellow glow. The air smelled of burning metal. The place was loud, and the employees looked pale and vaguely ill in the lighting. Above the floor on a far wall were offices and potted ferns behind a vast plate glass window that looked like it had never been cleaned.

"We acquired the plant sixteen months ago," the TTM analyst shouted over the din of clanging metal. "Less than 2% annual growth for well over a decade. It's just been sitting here, waiting for someone to spank it into shape."

The analyst led Steve up the staircase to the offices where they could look over the entire assembly process. In the peaceful, air conditioned quiet of the offices, the analyst gave Steve a few more numbers. Then he added, "It's a deceptively complicated job. A lot of moving parts."

"How many moving parts?" Steve asked.

"You've got a team of engineers under you, a design team, assembly line personnel, installation crews, a sales team, vendors … All of these pinwheels is what makes it so challenging to manage." The analyst paused. "These guys make sprinkler systems. They make them at a certain price. We want you to lead these people so that they make a better product for less. Like any investor, we're looking for wider margins. Far wider margins …"

With that everyone laughed.

"A lot of moving parts," Steve said, looking out over the dingy assembly floor.

"If we can't get those margins," the analyst went on, "then we're going to unload the entire operation."

"Not that we could find a buyer," the VP added.

"Somebody at the office mentioned razing the building and putting rental storage units here. Absolutely no moving parts. Real simple. Great ROI."

Steve took off his hardhat and then turned and stared out over the sea of industrial gloom. He then turned back to the analyst, who was nodding his head, smiling.

"Have you ever done anything like this before?"

"Never."

"It's a huge challenge," he said. "If you can do that, you can do anything. But it's a huge job."

"It is," Steve said. "But I'm going to have to talk it over with Susan."

"With who?"

"With my wife."

9

A Different World

Susan was putting Sarah to bed when Steve came home that night. Once their daughter was asleep, he sat down with his wife at the kitchen table and told her about the new job. He left nothing out. He told her about the acetylene soot, the yellow windows, the gloomy light, the gloomier employees. He told her about the likelihood that the entire plant would "just go away" if he failed to turn the operation around. He also told her about how the challenge excited him in a way he hadn't known in his professional life. If he succeeded, he could write his own ticket.

In spite of the strong equivocal note in Steve's voice, Susan took his hand in hers, and said, "I'll support whatever decision you make."

"In the long run, I think it might be the best decision for you, me and the baby," Steve said.

Later that month Steve and Susan closed on a house out on Long Island with a backyard and a swing. The 2,500-square-foot Cape Cod was eight miles from the plant where Steve could make his commute in ten minutes. On that first commute, within the air conditioned comfort of his well appointed Plymouth, all of the reservations Steve had had were momentarily absent.

For nine of those ten minutes, his mind was seized by fantasy. He saw himself developing a workforce that did not require supervision. He saw his people coming to work, doing their jobs exceedingly well without having someone tell them how to do them. Nobody asked about their fifteen minute morning break, nobody complained about the occasional thirty-minute lunch or the shortened afternoon break when business was good. He imagined himself announcing to the TTM board that he was about to knock out an entire layer of supervisors because he had this self-motivated, self-disciplined assembly force. He had trained his people personally and they would do as instructed … And then the fantasy abruptly faded as he pulled into the Gunther Company's litter-strewn parking lot.

When Steve entered the plant on his own for the first time, he saw vivid evidence of all the personal and operational complexities he would be confronted with. The assembly floor was a maze of pipes and fittings, the welding stations battered with heavy use and blatant neglect. Steve himself was younger than everyone by at least a decade, and he realized that he knew absolutely nothing about the fire suppression/sprinkler business. Then a man in his mid fifties who looked like a former Big Ten linebacker approached. As he stuck out a big grimy hand, Steve suddenly recognized him behind his safety glasses. He was Ivan Kowalski, the plant manager.

"Are you lost?" he asked.

"I'm Steve the new general manager."

"I know who you are," Ivan said. "We met before you took the job."

"I remember."

"You're young," Ivan said with a smile.

"NYU was a while ago," was all Steve would say to that.

"You're younger than my son."

Steve would mind his tongue, as he sensed that Ivan Kowalski was the least of his troubles. With mounting concern, Steve was coming to suspect that he would be surrounded by people who had no interest whatsoever in pleasing him. They would do their job with benign indifference, and leave the moment the whistle sounded. They would not lift a finger to help him succeed, even if it meant securing their livelihood. And so he politely bade farewell to Ivan Kowalski and ascended the metal staircase to his office.

Steve opened the door with his name on it, sat behind the vast metal desk, and stared at the twenty-year-old drapes. The drone of the assembly process was cancelled by the soundproof windows, and the smell of flux and acetylene soot cleansed by the vigorous air conditioning. So he sat there, drumming the desks surface with his knuckles.

◆   ◆   ◆

The following morning, Steve invited the people who would be reporting directly to him into his office for an 11 a.m. meeting. At 11:05 a.m., the head of supplies, the head of the sales team, marketing, the installation crew chief, the chief engineer, the company's CFO, and of course the plant manager, Ivan Kowalski, all filed in. They stood against the wall and plate glass window, either nervously looking about, or staring directly at Steve with an expression of deep fatigue. Steve noted that they were not commiserating with one another, not communicating in any way. Kowalski just stood there glowering at Steve. He looked as though he'd like to cut his heart out and eat it for lunch.

Hoping to start off his relationship with his people on a note of candor, he told them why he had been brought in.

"I'm here to make our product better, faster, and cheaper," he began. "Our chief concern, of course, is with productivity."

"You need more people to get more done," Kowalski interrupted.

"That doesn't increase productivity," Steve said. "We need to work harder and *smarter* to do that."

Kowalski rolled his eyes. No one else in the room was buying what Steve had to sell either.

"You don't know this business," Kowalski said, "until you've assembled the pipe."

"It isn't all about welding pipe, Ivan," the installation chief replied. "Especially pipes that leak at the elbows."

Kowalski didn't respond. He looked as though he'd heard this complaint untold times.

"I don't know this business," Steve went on. "What's more, I'm going to have to learn it from all of you." Steve paused for a moment. He was about to say something to the effect that he was the student and they were the teachers. But in that instant he decided to take that idea a good step further. "I am completely dependent upon each and every one of you. I want you to understand that."

This last statement got everyone's attention. Who was this guy in the suit, and why was he saying something like this? Just then the noon whistle sounded, and the room began to fidget. Steve understood that he had lost their attention, and called a quick end to the meeting just as the last of his people were filing out of the room.

10

The Student

Steve realized that he had not one but two serious problems. The first and most daunting was the fact that his employees were openly contemptuous of one another. They didn't communicate, didn't discuss ideas, hardly even pretended to work together as a team.

Kowalski had rudely put his finger on Steve's second problem: he knew nothing about this business. But his problem ran deeper than that. He suddenly realized that he worked for a communications conglomerate made up of thousands of brilliant employees who, like him, knew nothing about the manufacturing of sprinkler systems. When he called his direct report at the New York office, he asked in passing who the vendor for the sprinkler heads was. The VP laughed airily.

"Talk to your supply guy," he said. "He'll know."

"I didn't want to have to ask him," Steve said.

"Trying to keep displays of ignorance to a minimum?"

"Something like that."

"Sorry," was his final the sarcastic reply. "Can't help you in that department."

One thing was clear to Steve. There would be no backup at headquarters, no friendly, knowledgeable voice to call on. Nobody there knew sprinkler systems, nobody there cared about them. They cared about their core business, which was running radio and television stations. To them, the Gunther Company was an investment, and a regrettable one at that.

His people at the plant were obviously not going to offer any support either. Even if they did, he realized that he would have a new problem on his hands. How do you learn from your employees and still remain in a position of authority?

Steve had no idea. Those who knew the business best were journeymen, long-standing employees like Ivan Kowalski who instinctively did not trust him. He sensed that the senior employees were afraid he was going to come in and make sweeping changes that would ultimately jeopardize their jobs which some of them had held for fifteen years. And who could blame them? Steve had all the earmarks of a boss on the verge of running a functioning business into the ground: a complete lack of understanding of the operation, coupled with enough authority to make disastrous decisions.

Steve's next order of business had to be to gain the trust of these people, and to gain it quickly. With this thought in mind, he came to work the following Monday in khakis and a polo shirt. In his office he had his bright yellow hardhat and crisp new coveralls. He looked ridiculous and he knew it. Nevertheless, at 9:00 a.m., just as Kowalski was coming into the building, his lunchbox swinging from his fist, he told his plant manager that he would be spending the day on the floor with him. Ivan was going to teach him how to assemble pipe.

"You've got to be joking," Ivan said.

"I need to learn this business, Ivan," Steve replied, "and you know it better than anyone."

"Have you ever had an oxy-acetylene torch go off in your face?" he asked.

"Never. But if that's what it takes to learn the business …"

"I've got a lot on my plate this morning," Kowalski mumbled.

"Let's get started."

"This isn't part of my job description."

"I would appreciate it, Ivan."

The plant manager gave Steve a sideways look.

Ivan spent four hours showing Steve how to fit pipe, cut pipe, thread pipe, screw fittings, weld fittings, move sections down the line as he looked over Steve's shoulder, making sure he did everything exactly right. By lunchtime Steve's back was a mass of lumbar pain, his hands blistered under the leather gloves, his face blackened with a greasy mix of sweat, flux and steel shavings. His hardhat was still a bright yellow.

At first, Kowalski took pleasure in Steve's discomfort. He laughed when Steve's coveralls momentarily ignited as the torch flame glanced across his sleeve, leaving him with a minor burn on his arm and a gaping hole in his smoldering cuff. But Kowalski was visibly impressed with how Steve worked through it all and how he kept up the pace of the work. He was most impressed by how quickly Steve grasped the nature of how the assembly process operated. By the end of his third day with Kowalski, Steve knew he had succeeded on two fronts:

1.) He had gained a working understanding of the assembly process.

2.) He had managed to do the dirtiest, most dangerous job in the plant.

Steve's perspective had changed as well. He had initially considered his plant manager a loose cannon. Kowalski, he had been sure, would do everything he could to sabotage whatever changes Steve was going to try to implement. He'd thought Ivan had made it to plant manager because he was only a little smarter than those he supervised—and a whole lot tougher. This was the kind of guy who would do whatever it took to maintain the status quo on the manufacturing floor. After a week in the plant manager's company, however, Steve realized he had been wrong. Kowalski, Steve now understood, was actually quite smart. And he was tough for a reason.

11

An Unlikely Mentor

Steve had replaced a fellow by the name of Jack Huxtable, the owner/operator who had started the company nearly twenty years earlier. Huxtable was a New England aristocrat from Kennebunkport with solid credentials as a my-way-or-the-highway kind of manager. Although he had paid his people well, he consistently refused to listen to their opinions. He simply did not want to hear what they had to say, and was famously condescending toward everyone—especially Kowalski. Not surprisingly, Huxtable rarely invested in technology or standard upgrades in equipment. The neglect had a magnifying effect, as this culture of contented stagnation extended beyond the physical plant itself, and trickled down through its chain of command.

Evidence of Huxtable's style was everywhere. Steve noted that the employees on the floor worked reasonably hard, but they'd become accustomed to being treated like children from the moment they walked through the plant doors—always asking permission to do something differently, never taking any initiative. Kowalski, Steve noted, often seemed like he could barely control routine, minor frustrations. He flew off the handle when oxygen tanks were depleted, and yelled at employees who asked simple questions. Steve guessed he behaved with his subordinates just like Huxtable himself had behaved toward him. As Steve worked with Kowalski, however, he was coming to suspect that his plant manager simply wanted to be taken seriously. When the noon whistle sounded for lunch, Steve invited him up to his office.

Kowalski appeared puzzled. "I usually eat in the cafeteria," he said.

"It's quiet in my office," Steve said. "We can talk there."

For the next half-hour they discussed what would make the product better when it came off the line. They discussed staff schedules, equipment upgrades that might make the assembly process more efficient. Steve suggested that they paint some of the equipment on the floor to, as he put it, "lift the gloom."

To Steve's surprise, Kowalski offered plenty of suggestions on every topic, and as they talked he grew more animated, gradually betraying his evolving opinion of his new boss. Ivan, Steve could see, wanted nothing more than to sit in the quiet office and talk about what made sense to him. Instead of being told how things would be, he was now telling his boss how things could be done better.

"This is nice," Kowalski said just before they headed back down to the floor. "It helps to get away from the noise for a few minutes."

Once Ivan left, Steve felt an immense wave of relief wash over him. His plant manager was on his side. Here, Steve discovered, was all the technical expertise he would ever need.

The following morning this general sense of goodwill was galvanized into true loyalty. This was the morning that Ivan didn't show up for work. Almost instantly, the assembly floor found itself in disarray; nothing was getting done, as Ivan was the only one who had directed traffic on the floor. By 10:30 a.m., his panicked assistant came up to Steve's office to tell him Ivan still hadn't arrived, and so Steve turned to his Rolodex to give his plant manager a call. Just then, Ivan appeared in the door.

"Where have you been?" Steve said in a slightly raised voice.

Steve could see that Ivan was in a state of deep distress. Something was terribly wrong.

"My sixteen-year-old was in a car accident on her way to school this morning," he said. "She's okay, but she has a broken collarbone."

"Where is she?"

"She's still at St. Elizabeth's," he said, "but she'll be discharged in an hour or so."

"You need to be with her, Ivan."

Kowalski looked up at Steve. It seemed as though he was trying to discern whether or not his boss was serious.

"Don't even think of staying," Steve added. "Just go."

"Are you sure?" Ivan asked as though he couldn't quite believe what he was hearing.

"Thanks to you, I can direct operations on the floor. So go."

With that, Steve knew who his most loyal ally was at the Gunther Company.

◆   ◆   ◆

The following Monday Steve moved on with what he was privately calling his "Learn-From-My-Subordinates" campaign. His next stop was the engineering and design department. As his people sat at the board table in the conference room, he asked the four-person team to give him a crash course on the various systems. He wanted to know how they worked and what new modifications were in the pipeline. Most of all, he wanted to know how their systems differed from those of their competitors.

That's when something strange happened. As Steve sat among the four engineers and designers, he felt the oxygen leaving the room. Charles, the chief engineer, yammered in a deafening monotone about how superior competing systems were to the Gunther system.

"They're really fantastic," he said like a satisfied customer in a television endorsement. "And God, are they reliable."

"That's great to hear, Charles," Steve replied.

Another engineer noted how the Gunther Company never seemed to have the budget, time, or, in his words, "the creative wherewithal" to develop something that developers would pay a premium for.

"Our system's the least expensive one on the market," Charles explained. "What I should say is that we're the least expensive system that satisfies local, state and federal regulations for fire suppression systems in high-rise buildings."

"That's what we're all about," one of the designers said. "Cheap and easy."

"Our customers," Charles said in conclusion, "are developers who have eyes only for the bottom line. So we stick with what's worked for us in the past."

"That's … *depressing*," Steve said.

His design team nodded in unison.

They were an easy group to read. All four were bright, each with ideas on how to make a particular aspect of the Gunther Company's product better. As Steve sat among them, he saw that they looked defeated. Their time and talents had been wasted on developing a standard procedure for moving pipe, installing pipe, installing sprinkler heads—and doing it all for less money. What they hadn't been given was the opportunity to do their core job, which, to Steve's mind, was to develop a superior product. The work they were doing was substantially below their capabilities.

Steve spent the following day with the team going over system improvements. He brought along Andy, the CFO, and Allen, his marketing chief. Steve saw that his four engineers were clearly up to the task of designing something far better than what the company presently had, perhaps even a system capable of generating a whole new level of sales. Steve's CFO pointed out that a more reliable system would save the company money.

"For instance," he said, "we pay huge insurance premiums because our systems tend to leak."

"How much more?" Steve asked.

"Probably three times what other companies pay."

Steve nearly choked on his coffee.

"Sometimes," the CFO went on, "they go off inadvertently, and in one case a system didn't go off at all during a fire. That problem was later resolved, but the first two problems have yet to be completely remedied."

"A quality system," the CFO said, "would yield insurance savings for the building's owner."

"The leaks aren't our deal," one of the engineers said defensively. "That's Ivan's problem to solve."

"It could be the installation team's problem," his colleague added.

Not wanting to get caught up in a blame game, Steve stopped the conversation right there.

"What about the false alarms?" he asked.

As they stood before him, all three engineers closed their eyes as they spoke over one another about the promise of a new computerized control panel. Steve surmised as they spoke over one another that they already had the solution to the problem. What they lacked was the green light and a fairly substantial budget allocation.

"What you're telling me is that we're manufacturing, selling, and installing something that sometimes works and sometimes doesn't," Steve interrupted.

"That's right," Charles answered.

"And everyone agrees that a newly designed computerized control panel would make us a whole lot more reliable."

"It would change everything."

"Then that's it," Steve said. "We aren't going to turn this company around until we have something more to offer the marketplace."

"So you want us to develop the new control panel?" Charles asked.

"Can you do it?" Steve asked.

For a moment Steve thought they were smiling at the prospect of coming to work each morning and developing something new. It had to be more exciting than what they were doing now, which was essentially extending the life of an obsolete technology in order to keep the company's financial head above water—a strategy that had just about run its course.

"It'll take some time," Charles said.

"How much time?" Steve asked.

"That's hard to say."

12

A New Direction

By the end of Steve's first quarter on the job, he had the rapport he wanted with his people. He also had a working understanding of the business. He was still missing the right product, efficient production, meaningful sales, and the large margins TTM was looking for him to produce. All of that was a very long way off.

Steve spent a full week with his sales team, and quickly came to realize how little they actually knew about the product they sold. They were successful because they were slick. But this group of six men and three women lacked any technical interest whatsoever, and Steve knew that their obvious disinterest had to impair sales. To remedy this, he announced that they would each do what he had been doing—spending time within each phase of production and design in order to get a working understanding of what they were selling. The decree was met with silence.

"All developers want is to get the required fire suppression in their buildings," the head of sales announced with disarming certainty.

"Not every builder thinks that way," Steve countered.

"They don't?" asked Katherine, one of the women on the team. "My customers want *affordable*."

Then Andy, the CFO, cleared his throat. "Don't insurance companies have a say on the equipment that keeps the buildings they insure from burning to the ground?"

"No one's ever sold a system to an insurance company," a sales associate said. "They sell them to builders."

"Maybe there's an opportunity we're overlooking," the marketing director said.

"*Why are you even here?*" Katherine asked in a raised voice.

"He's here because I asked him to be here," Steve interjected.

"I'm just making a suggestion, Katherine," Andy protested.

"We're looking to expand our customer base," Steve said over all of their voices, "by developing a more reliable product. And marketing is going to let the insurance companies know it.

"This company has been growing less than 2% per year," he went on. "For the past three years the industry has been growing at 15%. So what's happening? Year after year our competitors have been taking away market share."

The sales team was silent.

"Might be good to catch up on new markets," Katherine conceded, "and take a look at what we're selling."

"It's a matter of survival," Steve added. "In business you either grow or you die."

◆   ◆   ◆

By the end of the following quarter, Steve began hearing the first grumblings from the TTM office that little or no progress was being made at the Gunther plant. One morning the VP called to schedule an appointment for that afternoon. The short notice gave the meeting an air of emergency.

"If this isn't going to work out," the VP told Steve, "we'll sell the plant and move on." He wasn't angry or disappointed in Steve's performance. He was just presenting facts.

"It isn't going to happen over night," was Steve's reply.

"Your bottom line is suffering," he said, gesturing to the balance sheets spread out before him. "Sales look like they'll be identical year-over-year, with expenses up 3%."

"I've had to add some costs to get things moving in the right direction."

"But you haven't added any volume."

"I haven't added any volume—*yet*."

"It's supposed to be the other way around," he said with a kindly smile. "You *cut* costs and *add* volume."

"Wait," Steve said, searching his breast pockets for a pen. "Let me write this down …"

The VP laughed. "How long before we see the numbers move?" he asked good-naturedly.

Steve couldn't say for sure. "A year. Eighteen months."

The VP parted his hands and said, "Wish it could happen sooner, but … good enough."

Apparently it wasn't good enough. The meeting at end of Steve's fourth quarter, the VP's tenor had changed. There was no kindly smile, no gentle jokes at Steve's expense. Another quarter had passed, he pointed out, and sales numbers were utterly identical. Steve urged further patience. The VP wearily shook his head.

"Patience is a commodity in very limited supply," he warned.

"What can I say?"

As Steve drove home that night, he felt the return of that familiar sense of panic.

He had never worked on a pass/fail basis before, and for the first time in his career he was actually frightened. "This is about wins and losses," he mumbled to himself. It wasn't about strategies people did or didn't like, or audits they didn't agree with. This was a brick-and-mortar company with three-hundred employees, and if things were not turned around, it was all going to go away, and Steve's career was going to go with it. His concern, of course, did not rest solely with his employees.

Over the course of the next month the anxiety only intensified. His sleep was fitful, his mind consumed with a hundred different strategies and a thousand different tactics for turning this company around. But he couldn't get any of his initiatives to yield any measurable results. All the work he had put into developing meaningful relationships with his employees seemed to have only made the atmosphere more pleasant each day. People were no longer shouting at each other. They were communicating with each other, actually sharing ideas. It was nice to be on friendly terms with everyone, but that was all his efforts had apparently amounted to. And that, Steve knew, was not enough.

13

Treading Water

Later that year, Charles, the head of the design team, poked his head in Steve's office and asked if he had a minute. Steve nodded, fatigue showing in his red-rimmed eyes.

Charles ambled into the office with a hand behind his back. Dangling from it, Steve saw, was a large circuit panel trailing a rooster tail of colored signal wires.

Charles smiled as he revealed the new panel.

"It's a prototype," Charles said. "It uses a computerized control panel—right here." He pointed to the column of switches, and then to the circuits on the opposite side. "It's manufactured by an upstart vendor right here on Long Island."

Not only was the product far better than what they were currently selling, it was less expensive to produce.

"We've been fiddling around with it for the past couple of years," Charles explained. "Huxtable wasn't sure this was the direction to go."

"So what exactly makes it better than what we have now?" Steve asked.

"Well, everything," Charles said. "It's more reliable, it's sleek. This technology used to cost more, but now it costs less."

Steve took the panel from Charles and noticed that it had a battery port.

"What's this for?" he asked.

"When you have a fire, the electricity eventually fails—sometimes sooner, sometimes later. But it almost always goes out. If it goes out before the system activates, then your building burns all the way to the ground."

"A selling point."

"If it was my high-rise," Charles said, "I wouldn't have a system without this in it."

"That's how we need to think," Steve said. "*'If it was my high-rise ...'*"

Steve accepted the panel from Charles like it was a precious gift.

"Looks like something we can build on?" he asked.

"Oh, yeah," the designer assured him. "Definitely something we can build on."

◆   ◆   ◆

In spite of the panel's great potential in the marketplace, Steve knew that it would require a great deal of change in the plant's personnel to bring it online. One of its primary benefits was that it could be assembled by fewer of Kowalski's people, which would instantly lower payroll. This would go a long way toward pacifying the corporate office. However, the layoffs would inevitably jeopardize Steve's relationships with the people who had helped him through a difficult year—and now he would be paying them back with pink slips. In any event, Steve needed a quick payback so that the company could become profitable sooner rather than later.

Steve took the prototype to his supply chief and asked him to organize the necessary vendors around the new panel. He then had the design team take the panel to the sales people, and had them demonstrate its virtues. Steve made sure his marketing director and CFO were present. They instantly saw the bigger picture, and were soon coming up with big ideas to match.

For all the sales team's slickness, they now understood exactly what they were looking at, and they understood how it would put money in their pockets. The insurance guys would now be on their side, pushing their product to the penny-pinching builder and the up-market builder alike. The Gunther Company, they saw, would soon have a dramatically improved product to offer. Steve called in his three-person marketing team to begin pumping out press releases and print ads in the various building trade journals to announce the news.

After researching his competitors products and prices, Steve was reasonably sure he could raise Gunther's prices by 25% and still be viewed in the industry as a bargain. The price increase could easily be recouped in insurance premium savings, and this is exactly how they would sell it. But first Steve had to attend to some unpleasant business.

The following day, he invited Kowalski up to his office over lunch to break the news. Ivan brought his lunchbox, sat down across from Steve's desk, and began to fill Steve in on assembly matters. The moment he saw that something was on Steve's mind—something important—he stopped talking.

"We're going to have to let some people go," Steve said.

"Whose people?"

"Your people."

Ivan set down his sandwich.

"I knew this was coming," Ivan said.

"I've got to cut costs in the short term," Steve said, "or we're out of business."

"So what are you getting at?"

"I'm getting significant pressure from the corporate office to either cut costs or dramatically raise revenues," Steve went on. "The panel will eventually bring in the revenues, but it's going to take a while."

"And you can cut costs right now," Kowalski said.

"That's right."

With that, Ivan stuffed his sandwich back into his lunchbox.

"There's only one thing I can say for sure," he said.

Steve braced himself for Ivan's wrath. He was about to get the surprise of his life.

"What's that?" he warily asked.

"You have this company's best interest at heart," Ivan said. "This isn't something that I think. It's something I know."

14

The Loyalist

Faced with uncertainty at every turn, Steve could be sure of only one thing: Ivan's loyalty. There was no mistake to be made. Ivan trusted Steve. Nobody wanted layoffs, but if Steve thought they were necessary, then that was the bottom line for Ivan.

But Steve wasn't going to take his plant manager for granted. On his desk he laid out the spreadsheets, which detailed revenues and expenses. He showed Ivan the memos he'd received from the corporate office telling him what was at stake if he didn't take immediate and dramatic action. In no uncertain terms, the TTM vice president who was overseeing the Gunther Company's progress stated that he was going to shut this operation down if Steve didn't act. Then Steve took this explanation of the situation one step further.

"This VP's not a bad guy," he said. "He's got to answer to people above him, and they've got to answer to the shareholders who own this company, people who don't want to see their retirement savings vanish just because we can't make this company profitable."

Steve then led Ivan through the balance sheets, explaining the principal aspects of the accounting, slowly painting a picture of fiscal collapse that, by the end of Steve's tour, was inescapable—even to someone as unfamiliar to accounting as Ivan Kowalski. Then he moved on to show Ivan what was happening at the TTM headquarters in the city, and finally what their competitors were doing. "If we don't evolve," Steve said, "we'll die. Everyone will be out of work."

Kowalski had his hands spread out across either side of the memos and balance sheets.

"I get it," he finally said.

"I'm sorry it has to be this way, Ivan. I really am."

The people who were going to lose their jobs, Ivan explained to Steve, would have their lives turned upside down, as it was a time in America when there were more workers than jobs. Ivan had one request: "If we explain the predicament to them," he said, "the way you explained it to me, then I think it would help take the sting out of the situation."

"Let's bring them up here right now."

◆   ◆   ◆

As painful as the layoffs were, they were only the beginning of Steve's problems. A few days later his VP called to say he and two TTM analysts would be dropping by the plant to see for themselves why it was taking so long to achieve the numbers. He wanted Steve to put together a presentation on what he was planning to do differently. He wanted specifics.

Steve locked himself away in his office for the rest of the day and that night, pulling it all together, outlining a grand strategy built around the new panel. Dramatic increases in revenue would be met though greater sales as a result of the improved panel. Marketing would be directed at insurance companies instead of solely at builders. Costs could be cut immediately through layoffs. Steve wanted to paint a very clear picture: money would be *saved* in the short term, and *made* over the long-term. In any case, the Gunther Company was on the verge of meaningful profitability.

Steve was asleep on his office sofa when his staff began arriving. He awoke with a start and began cleaning himself up in the lavatory. When the VP and the analysts arrived an hour later, Steve was ready for them.

They sat at one end of the folding board table as Steve led them through the numbers, which, by his own admission, made for a straight line.

"A flat line," the analyst remarked. "Like a dead man's EKG."

"I have a plan to revive the patient."

"But it's going to take time, right?" the VP said.

The analyst and the VP exchanged a brief, knowing look.

"Look, Steve," the VP said. "I understand what you're up against. But frankly, it ... looks like a lot of work."

"I don't follow you."

"Look at this place," he said, indicating the dingy office, his metal desk, the particleboard table they were working on, the Eisenhower-era drapes.

"Frankly," one of the analysts said, "it looks like more trouble than it's worth. And the potential for a meaningful return on TTM's investment is, well, minimal."

"I understand your frustrations."

"Steve, it just looks like you're falling behind," the VP said.

"Again, I understand what you're saying," Steve countered.

The meeting ended a few seconds later, and Steve didn't feel good about how it had gone. But he knew in his bones that he was on the right track. The one point that bothered him, however, was the VP's observation that it looked as though he was "falling behind." It bothered him because he knew that it wasn't true. Steve wasn't selling TTM on the pipedream of a breakthrough. He actually believed it.

◆   ◆   ◆

So Steve hunkered down. In the weeks before the new system was to come online, he became a salesman. He saw himself as a shy personality, someone who probably wasn't going to be the most productive salesman off the mark. But he knew the product better than anyone else on the sales team, and he believed he had a strategy for selling it: make it all about saving money for the customer. The new systems cost more, but savings in insurance premiums would pay for the difference within two years. He had to make it so that the choice for potential customers was obvious.

The strategy worked.

Not only did it work, it worked from the very beginning. Orders began flowing in within a month of the sales initiative. The sales team had nearly doubled their commissions, and they were now more motivated than they had ever been in their professional lives. A trade journal promoted the new system in a press release Allen put together, and now there was a growing sense out there that the Gunther Company was gunning to become an industry leader in—of all categories—quality and innovation. Meanwhile, Steve was able to put together his revenue projections in his new budget, which, Steve thought, would get some attention from the corporate office when they saw them. The day after he submitted his budget he got a call from the VP.

"What's up with these numbers, Steve?" he asked.

"They're real," Steve said.

"You have sales doubling in the next year."

"There's a reason for that."

"Well," he said, "what's the reason?"

Steve laughed. "We expect to place twice as many orders over the next twelve months."

"That, my friend, is an excellent reason."

Book II

15

Andreas

Steve sat back in his office chair and contemplated the events of the past two years. Eventually he was struck by an epiphany:

Through this entire process, he thought, I did not develop a single system. I did not assemble or install an entire system. Nor did I market one. All I did was organize and support the people who could do it all for me. That, he realized, was the core of his job.

Suddenly Steve's career seemed to be coming full circle. His name began appearing in squibs and business briefs of the *Wall Street Journal, Fortune*, and *The Economist.* Given his limited experience, this was something of a surprise. Out of the blue he was being touted by people in the New York business community as "a brilliant analyst," "a gifted strategist," *and* "a remarkable general manager." His series of successes had an appealing diversity, which set him apart from the thousands of other brilliant young businessmen and businesswomen of New York City.

What further intrigued business page reporters and editors was the deep sense of loyalty the Gunther Company employees expressed for their boss. Down through the ranks they all loved Steve. They'd all been to his house, they all had met Susan. Some of their children had even babysat for his daughter. The composite picture was that of a young general manager who had somehow harnessed that loyalty and channeled it in the service of salvaging a dying company. Now the company was thriving, with Steve's employees gaining self-esteem and becoming proud of their work. As his people became more confident, they became more proficient, and the company's reputation was enhanced. As a result of this young businessman's humble approach, he was able to re-instate previously laid-off employees at a time when the local economy was shedding them at a heartbreaking rate. He was expecting to be adding another dozen jobs to the payroll by the end of the year.

Regional politicians and local civic leaders were singing Steve's praises. Business page reporters loved his down-at-heel nature, never failing to note that he called his subordinates "my people." Photographers focused their lenses on the block-letter banner put up over the assembly floor: "WE DON'T SAVE BUILDINGS. WE SAVE LIVES." And they all loved the ugly drapes in his office, the stories of Steve cleaning the restrooms and cafeteria himself, of how he learned to work with a welding torch in his first weeks as general manager. In a harsh business climate, Steve had staked his business success to the idea of teamwork and a sense of community. The media stories and their accompanying pictures were always the same: Steve sat smiling behind his cluttered desk, while the headline read: "A new breed of leader."

◆   ◆   ◆

Then came the day when Steve received a call from someone he had only read about but never met. His name was Andreas Zimmerman, a bona fide international business tycoon who had recently arrived in Manhattan from Dusseldorf, Germany, and who was reported to be worth in excess of $1.2 billion. "Andreas," as everyone on Wall Street had come to refer to him, spoke five languages, wore tiny, silver-framed architect glasses, hand-tailored silk suits, sleek ties, and had a widely-reported affection for Persian cats. Few in New York knew much about him, and those who did found him to be over-the-top as far as his public image was concerned. He presented himself to the world as the enigmatic European genius with an aristocratic lineage—the great grandson of a Prussian duke and the son of a multi-millionaire businessman. The son had turned the father's millions into a billion-plus, and he was now in the United States looking to enhance the family empire.

Andreas was a peculiar but interesting character. The *London Times* had recently referred to the acquisitive Zimmerman as an "intellectual machine," while the *Daily Telegraph* pronounced him to be "one of the great entrepreneurs of his generation." Now, in his late forties, Andreas was six-feet three inches tall with fine blonde hair. He had a Gulf Stream that ferried him to and from the European continent, and it was available to him at a moment's notice. His nemesis, the *New York Post*, often likened him to the quintessential James Bond villain.

While Wall Street saw Andreas as a bit of a caricature of the international businessman, he was nevertheless someone to be reckoned with. He courted the press, and was said to hold the equivalent of masters degrees in several fields of study from prestigious German and French universities. He rented an entire quarter-floor in the World Trade Center, which he had refurbished at outlandish expense. The walls were cherry wood, the floor tiles inlaid with marble quarried from an ancient German monastery destroyed in the war. You could see the Statue of Liberty from every exterior window of his palatial office. But his office was not warm. Steve recalled reading somewhere that Andreas Zimmerman was "addicted to gadgets."

◆   ◆   ◆

No one could have been more surprised than Steve when his secretary left a note that Andreas Zimmerman's office had called. When Steve called back, Andreas's secretary explained that Mr. Zimmerman was currently in Brussels and would be returning to New York on Monday.

"He would like to meet with you in the afternoon," she went on in her faint German accent. "Six o'clock would be best."

The appointment was made. But it had been made with the air of a command, Steve couldn't help but notice, rather than that of a request. And he had only a vague idea of what it could be about. He nevertheless suspected that Andreas Zimmerman was going to try to hire him away from his baby, his little Long Island sprinkler plant.

When Steve called Irwin to get his take on the meeting, his old friend confirmed his suspicions.

"He's read one of those stories about you in the *WSJ*," Irwin said with certainty.

"All I know is that he's a wealthy investment banker."

"An investment banker who runs five miles every morning before he goes to the office," Irwin added. "He's one of those people who has to be the best at everything he does—whether it's bridge, croquet or business."

"The call got my attention."

"How much is TTM paying you to run that plant?"

Steve told him.

"Let me tell you this, my friend," Irwin said with a knowing chuckle. "Andreas is going to make you an offer that you are going to find very difficult to refuse."

The following Monday Steve arrived at his 6:00 p.m. appointment and was instantly reminded of just how far removed his world was from the world of Andreas Zimmerman. The office was the most lavish Steve had ever seen, with its plush maroon carpeting, marble statuary, and staggering views of Staten Island. The Statue of Liberty rose up out of New York Harbor in brilliant 3-D relief.

Andreas's secretary greeted Steve with a firm handshake. Her hair was very short, her business suit sharply creased, her lipstick very precisely applied.

"Mr. Zimmerman," she said, "will see you in a moment." She then offered Steve a seat next to a framed feature story on Andreas that had been clipped from NEWSWEEK. The young venture capitalist stood before the Eiffel Tower under a headline that introduced him as "Europe's New Kid on the Block."

Five minutes later Mr. Zimmerman was finally ready to see him. The secretary led Steve down a short hallway to a towering pair of doors that parted and then gave way to a corner office where Andreas sat behind a vast desk of polished mahogany. Steve was offered a seat beside the desk where Andreas sat, legs crossed, hands folded on a kneecap, eyes studying Steve for a long moment. He seemed a good deal warmer than Steve had anticipated.

"You have quite a reputation," Andreas began. "You've done so much for this little company."

Steve shrugged and thanked him.

"So what do you attribute your success to?" Andreas asked.

The question caught Steve a little off guard. He thought for a moment before saying: "Realizing that my success was dependant on all of the people in the company."

"Dependent upon whom exactly?"

"Dependant upon everyone," Steve said. "From the top right on down the line."

"Surely your success wasn't attached to *everyone*," Andreas said, as though he couldn't quite believe how Steve answered the question.

"You have to bear a couple of things in mind," Steve said. "I took on that job knowing absolutely nothing about the business," Steve said. "Nothing whatsoever."

Zimmerman smiled, clearly impressed by Steve's candid and clear analysis of his own success.

"You make it sound very simple," he said. "But I know it's not."

"You're right. It wasn't simple."

Andreas smiled warmly, and then abruptly straightened himself in his chair.

"Let me get to the point," he said. "I am buying a restaurant chain, and I would like you to run it for me."

Steve felt his eyes go dry. Irwin was right, he thought.

"I intend to keep it for about five years," Zimmerman went on. "When it becomes profitable, I plan to flip it. Currently the business is struggling. It will be a huge challenge for you if you are will to take the job I'm offering. But I have absolutely no doubt whatsoever that you are up to that challenge."

And then Andreas stopped talking. He just sat for a moment and watched Steve take it all in.

"Perhaps you could elaborate a little more," Steve said

"It would be similar to what you faced at the Gunther Company," Andreas replied very slowly, "only much larger."

"How much larger?"

"You could say that, in a sense, it would be approximately 830 times larger."

The company he would be heading up, Andreas explained, was Antonio's Italian Restaurants, an 830-unit up-market restaurant chain that had been struggling in recent years. There were some 1,300 people at the Manhattan headquarters, and restaurants scattered all across North America. Steve and Susan had actually been to one out on Long Island, and had liked it well enough to have returned once or twice. But Steve had no idea of the nature of the company's problems, and Andreas wasn't inclined at the moment to discuss them in any detail. All he would offer was a single remark: "You'll probably need to restructure before you do anything."

"I understand," Steve replied.

"I am convinced that you are the person to turn this company around."

"What's your ultimate goal for the company?" Steve asked.

"I want to improve its bottom line," Andreas said, "and then I want to sell it. I used to do this with Goldman-Sachs's money, and now I do it with my own."

"That's an ambitious plan."

"If you can turn it around in five years," Andreas said very slowly, "I will give you 30% of the value you create. In the meantime, you'll receive a salary several times what you are earning now."

Alas, here was the offer Irwin had been talking about.

16

Starting Over

Before accepting, Steve visited a dozen or so of the franchise restaurants and conducted a thorough study of the company books. He took a close look at the P&L statements, and saw that the company was slowly bleeding money. Nearly every single trend was in the wrong direction.

Above all else, Steve wanted to see if he felt comfortable with the company. This wasn't something he could measure quantitatively. He just wanted to get a sense of its underlying character; he wanted to be comfortable with the organization, as his father would say, "in his gut." One night he, Susan and their daughter went out to the local Antonio's. Although it was the peak dinner hour, the restaurant was hardly busy. To his untrained eye, Steve noted that the menu appeared cluttered, and the help seemed sluggish. Susan agreed. "But the food is pretty good," she said.

"You're right," Steve confessed with a smile. "I have no idea what I'm talking about."

Steve understood the gravity of this move. He'd be making a lot more money, and there would be the chance for a payday of a magnitude that would allow him real financial freedom. All he needed to do was fix another broken company in a business he knew nothing about. The thought of failure elicited a vague sense of panic, and a haunting memory of his first days of tribulation at the Gunther Company. Everything was at stake. Again, this could prove to be either a career killer or a dream maker.

The following weekend Steve drove his family down the Eastern Seaboard, and each night they went out to a different Antonio's. He and Susan tried to note the differences in the quality of menus, service and facilities, but came away with only a short list of things they didn't particularly like. After dinner on their last night in Norfolk, Virginia, Steve turned to Susan, set his napkin in his lap, and said, "Well, I think I'm ready."

"Then it's time to call Mr. Zimmerman," she replied.

"I think it is."

◆   ◆   ◆

Andreas was standing in front of his desk when Steve greeted him, towering over him in a way that almost seemed to be an act of intimidation. Then he broke into a broad smile.

"I'm assuming you have something you want to tell me?"

"There is."

Right then and there, Steve decided that people were wrong about Andreas Zimmerman.

"You know," Andreas went on. "There's something I wanted to show you." He then turned to his desk, offered Steve a seat, and produced a large book with an ornately tooled leather cover. When Andreas opened it, Steve could see it was a photo album.

"I wanted to show you my family," Andreas said. "I have a beautiful wife. Her name is Greta, and we have two little girls ... Here they are."

Steve felt an extraordinary sense of warmth in the moment. It was a moment of privilege. Andreas was taking a page from Steve's playbook, and he wanted Steve to know it. Zimmerman was a famously private, even secretive business-man, and here he was opening up his life, giving Steve a favored glimpse. Zim-merman's was a glamorous world of luxury yachts, exotic locales, and palatial homes. In one photo Margaret Thatcher was bouncing his daughter on a knee; in another Henry Kissinger kissed his wife on her cheek. As Steve leafed through the pages, Andreas asked about his wife and daughter, and wondered if he had any pictures. From his wallet Steve produced an accordion of family photos, which Andreas seemed to study carefully, as though they were beautiful balance sheets.

"So" Andreas said, looking up from the photos, "let's make it official."

"I'm here to accept the job," Steve said.

Zimmerman stood and placed two hands on Steve's shoulders. "I think this is going to work out exceedingly well."

"I couldn't be more confident," Steve said. "There's just one thing ... I'm going to need a full month to oversee a smooth transition at the Gunther Com-pany."

"That won't work," Andreas said flatly. "I'll need you to begin in a few days' time."

Suddenly Steve felt a pang.

"I can't do that," Steve said. "We've made one enormous change after another there, and I don't want my departure to destabilize the entire operation."

"I just don't see how—"

"I need a month," Steve interrupted.

Andreas paused and appeared to be sizing up the man who would be running his newest and largest acquisition. His down-turned eyes suggested that he was not pleased.

"Okay," Andreas said. "You have your month."

17

Back to School

Steve arrived early at the Gunther plant and flopped down in the chair behind his desk. As his people filed in, the familiar din of activity grew and grew. Prematurely overcome with nostalgia, he thought of how much he loved this place. He even said it aloud: "I love this place." But, he reminded himself, it was time to move on.

Ivan came in a few minutes later looking a little harried, his mind consumed with the details of the business of the day. Then he noticed that something wasn't quite right. Steve was just sitting there, not looking him in the eyes.

"What's going on?" he asked.

Steve didn't say anything right away because he didn't know how to say it.

"Ivan, I'm going to be leaving."

What are you talking about?" Ivan asked.

"I'm leaving the Gunther Company. I've been offered another job."

What followed was an anguished appeal for Steve to change his mind. "This place will collapse without you," Ivan said. "You're indispensable to this operation …"

"Ivan," Steve interrupted, "the graveyards are filled with indispensable people."

"You just can't leave … look at everything we've accomplished together … this was a failing company, and now it's a little powerhouse …"

But Steve was leaving, and Ivan knew it. Once the shock had worn off, Steve told him that he was going to recommend that Ivan take his job. If he didn't, Steve warned, everything they'd accomplished really might be jeopardized.

"Mark my words," Steve began. "If you don't get the job, a new guy will come in and try to validate himself by exaggerating the smallest problems, and then 'fix' them. He'll put me down and everything I did here, and he'll put you down too. The last thing he'll do is cast himself as the savior of this company."

"Please don't go."

"Ivan," Steve said, "you can handle it. And besides, I've already made my decision."

◆   ◆   ◆

Six weeks later Steve moved his family into a beautiful house in Westchester County. He then set about his plan, which, in effect, was to rehabilitate the broken rapport with the many franchise owners who had felt abandoned by the parent company in recent years. He resolved to stick with what he knew: building solid relationships with the people around him, which he would harness to drive business in a new and more profitable direction. He would learn the technical details of the franchise business as he went along.

Steve's initial sense of what was ailing this company came from a shocking story he read in the *New York Post*. It was about Andreas. "To describe Andreas Zimmerman as aloof," the story read, "is to describe Shanghai as a village in China." Zimmerman was the most aloof human being this associate editor had ever encountered.

Stories of Andreas were legendary, and the article recounted several shocking accounts. Only recently Andreas had fired thirteen of his VPs and four general managers in a single morning. Andreas was accustomed to conducting business from 40,000 feet, keeping himself isolated in his office, from his chalet in the Swiss countryside, or from the satellite telephone on his yacht. If the results he expected were not met, he was known to fire CEOs by telephone as well.

In Steve's limited exposure to his boss, Andreas had made an effort to be warm and personal, and it didn't seem like an act. But now Steve wondered if he hadn't been played. It was at this point that he sensed a return of the familiar old panic.

Steve tried to shake off the anxiety, but it wouldn't really go away. He had made his bed, and now he was going to have to sleep in it. So he contemplated his initial approach … How was he going introduce himself to the people around him? What was the very first step he would take? A very small handful of ideas came to him. A very small handful, indeed.

If Steve was going to succeed in turning this company around, he was going to have to present himself as a radically different kind of leader to everyone in the company. He was not Andreas Zimmerman. But the company, he realized, was huge. They included not only the employees at headquarters, but 800-plus franchise owners evenly scattered across the country. With that thought in mind, Steve decided to embark on an extended road trip. He would visit as many of the franchise owners as he possibly could, and he was going to listen to them to get their take on what was right, what was wrong, and what needed to be fixed. They were the experts. They were his Ivan Kowalskis.

18

Point of View

That night Steve sat down with Susan at their dining room table and charted a course that would take him first to New England, then to the upper Midwest, the Northwest, down the Pacific coast, across the South and finally up the eastern seaboard. Two days later he was underway, traveling by air and by rental car, dropping out of the sky and then driving from one restaurant to another, visiting with owner after owner in a booth over coffee. Everywhere he went the complaint was the same: Antonio's headquarters was not listening to its franchise owners. Meanwhile, they were constantly being hit up for unfunded mandates that demanded that they buy everything from new ovens to new lighting to new carpeting. In some cases the mandates were actually pushing owners toward bankruptcy. Some appeared despondent.

"Seven years ago I had a flourishing business," a Dallas franchisee nearly shouted at Steve, "and people came because of the menu. Then the menu changed, and I was told to either change with the company or sell the business ... *What kind of company demands that!*"

The angriest complaints were directed at those responsible for the recent marketing and advertising campaigns. The spots were, by any standard, lifeless and ineffective. The consensus among franchise owners was that they were so inane and tasteless that they actually drove business away.

Steve had seen the ads, and secretly knew that the owners had a point. The newest crop of television campaigns were beyond bad, featuring a white-bread suburban family ordering spaghetti dishes from a buck-toothed sixteen-year-old server with an acne problem. There was nothing "Italian" about the pieces, nothing that held any allure. A similar piece that had aired a year earlier was lampooned on the Tonight Show for its sheer corniness, and now, with this new piece, the franchise owners had seen enough. They were prepared to mutiny if something wasn't done.

On the final leg of Steve's tour, he resolved to analyze and isolate the problem in the marketing and advertising departments. Steve had yet to introduce himself to his staff, but this, he knew, had to be the first order of business.

Steve's first day on the job at the corporate headquarters was taken up with meetings of introduction with department heads and his own staff. Steve's first impression was that the people here were in a deep funk. It occurred to him that, in a strange way, the staff was a little chagrined to be working for this outfit. There was a lack of energy, a sense of being generally *beleaguered*. He often over-heard people say things to the effect that one restaurant chain or another "has really got their act together ..." Steve's people had been beaten up so regularly by their own franchisees that they were now content to just make it through another day. Ironically, the only exception to this rule was with the ad team. After a meeting with the department heads, Steve came to see them as a hardworking and creative crew of eighteen men and women. They knew how to bring all the ingredients together in an efficient manner, but they felt their work was all for naught, as it was regularly sabotaged by poor execution and by the franchisees themselves.

"They aren't doing their part," a department head brooded.

"We're going to look at every aspect of the business," Steve replied. "I promise you. We will fix it."

"There's a whole lot of work to be done."

To Steve's bewilderment, the marketing department was probably the most organized team in the company. When Steve met with Tom, the chief marketing director, he didn't pretend that his team was doing great work.

"At times I think we try too hard to please everyone," Tom explained to Steve in a closed-door meeting. "But in the end we haven't been able to please anyone."

"I have to be honest," Steve said, taking special care not to antagonize his marketing executive. "The franchise owners are not happy with marketing and advertising."

"I'm aware of the unhappy owners, but I always tell them we're doing our best here with a very—and I mean a *very*—limited budget."

"Maybe now would be a good time to go over the numbers together," Steve said.

As it turned out, Tom was not exaggerating.

As he led Steve through the marketing and advertising balance sheets it became all too clear that a large portion of the blame lay with the genius who thought this was an adequate budget for an 830-restaurant franchise. Tom had money for a smattering of television and radio spots, with the remaining sliver of his budget going toward production costs. If the budget was tripled, Steve thought to himself, it wouldn't be enough, and this poor bastard has been left to twist in the wind.

So the picture grew more complex as Steve's analysis developed. This was not going to be a simple matter of replacing an incompetent marketing officer. The more deeply Steve looked into what Tom had accomplished with what he had, the more he saw that this guy knew how to stretch a dollar. Unfortunately it had been stretched much too far, and the company's excessive frugality had come back to haunt it in a big way.

What concerned Steve was the fact that it had been the franchise owners who had roundly turned down Tom's request to modestly redraw the contract between the parent company and the franchisees, which would bring it within the current industry norms. The change in the contract centered around a small increase in the percentage of gross revenues franchisees paid the parent company, which went toward the marketing and advertising budget; and now they were complaining about the results of their own penny-wise, pound-foolish approach. The franchise owners were running the show on the one hand—and criticizing it mercilessly on the other. They simply didn't know what was good for them.

The following morning Steve met with Andreas at his office where they discussed Steve's initial impressions, as well as his preliminary "diagnosis," as Andreas called it, of what was keeping the company from performing as it should.

"We all know the franchisees are unhappy," Steve began. "And their biggest complaint—"

"Is with marketing and advertising," Andreas said, finishing his sentence. "Yes, I know. We need to address this right away. It should be our first priority."

"Marketing is grossly under-funded," Steve remarked.

"And grossly under-talented."

"I'm convinced that they have the talent. What they don't have is money."

"There are 830 owners who have no interest bumping up the budget for a slew of absurd commercials. This is a no-brainer. I already know what needs to happen."

"If the owners could be shown that it's in their best interest to let our people do what they do best …"

"But it's not in their best interest."

"We need to look long and hard at that assumption."

Steve was careful not to present his opinions as a challenge. Andreas, however, seemed to take some kind of offense to Steve's persistence.

"Well then, what's your brilliant idea?"

"At the very least, the updated contract needs to resemble other contracts within the industry," Steve said. "If the owners can kick in their fair share, and corporate could take on a higher ad budget, the ads we could then buy would definitely have an effect on the bottom line."

"Perhaps it's worth a look," Andreas allowed.

Steve came away from the meeting with a vague sense of dread. Andreas had made up his mind as to what was wrong with the company. Steve didn't want their relationship to devolve into one in which Steve saluted Andreas and carried out his orders. Then again, perhaps Steve had misinterpreted his new boss's intention. He replayed the conversation he'd just had over and over in his mind, and reminded himself that it had ended with Andreas giving way to Steve's insistence that they reconsider the contract and budgets. By the end of the day, Steve had convinced himself that Andreas was an enlightened boss. Indeed, he was the kind of boss Steve had always hoped to one day have the privilege of working for.

19

A Broken Team

As the weeks passed, Andreas's tendency to micromanage gradually came to bear. As unwelcome as the intrusion was for Steve, it was, at times, reassuring. Once again, Steve had found himself at the head of another business he knew absolutely nothing about. But unlike his experience at the Gunther Company, he now had an interested and involved chief who was somewhat more knowledgeable of the industry than he was. Andreas's presence, as overbearing as it could be, offered a measure of confidence—at least in the beginning.

Two months into the new job, Steve scheduled a meeting with Tom, the CMO, and the heads of the various corporate teams. The purpose of the meeting was to discuss openly and comprehensively what was wrong, and what could be done to remedy the situation as a whole. It just happened to fall on a Friday.

"Should I pack my belongings beforehand?" Tom asked Steve.

"Absolutely no need," Steve said. "I give you my word."

The meeting convened at 9:30 a.m. in the conference room. The eighteen staff members quietly filed in with coffee cups, briefcases and notepads. Steve stood near the door, greeting each person as he or she came in, each puzzled by his good humor and relaxed smile. When Tom came in, he had a look of deep anxiety—in spite of Steve's reassurances. He looked as though he hadn't slept the night before.

Once everyone was seated, Steve introduced himself to the group, and explained the purpose of the conference as he stood before a flip-chart he'd set up at one end of the table.

"I have a presentation that I've spent the last few days putting together," he began, "and I want anyone to jump in wherever they think they can illuminate a particular area of our marketing and advertising effort."

Steve watched on as just about every person in the room exchanged a knowing look across the table. It was a look of relief. Perhaps they would be allowed to keep their jobs after all.

Just as Steve was about to start his presentation, he paused and reconsidered what he was about to say.

"The purpose of this meeting," he said, "is simple. I brought you all here so that you can teach me how to run a customer trial in a restaurant chain."

The remark produced a ripple of laughter across the table.

"I know absolutely nothing about this business," he continued. "But you do. It's a very complex business model, and I want you to know one thing. I am depending upon each one of you to show me how to become effective in this industry."

Steve let the admission settle in. Then he resumed, just as he had at the Gunther Company, moving through the recent history of the various radio and television campaigns, the dwindling budgets, and the general flattening of company revenues. As Steve proceeded, he sensed the room growing restless. He wasn't glossing over the sad trajectory of failure, nor was he pointing fingers. The head of one marketing task force interrupted him in order to blame the advertising agency the company had hired which had produced, in his words, "the most absurd television ad in the history of advertising." The problem was, he went on, "a failure to execute his team's original vision."

This elicited an angry counterattack by the advertising executive, who saw fit to blame "the moron who drew up the marketing and advertising budget" that had yanked 30% of his money out from under his feet *after* his ads had gone into production. The marketing task force chief responded with a personal assault, and accused Tom of being "a flaming idiot." Within seconds the room was a beehive of acrimony, which Steve ended by shouting to the room to "Go back to your corners!" Once the room had quieted down, he added in a calm voice, "This isn't about blame. This is about coming up with a marketing plan that works."

So everyone began again, this time with Steve leading them calmly and deliberately, step-by-step, through each decision that was made in the process of creating these truly atrocious television and radio ads. By noon Steve saw patterns emerging. They mostly had to do with creative changes made after production had begun. In each case, the changes were for the worse, and nearly all of them prompted by "strong recommendations" from a specific franchise owner who thought he knew better than anyone on the team as to what constituted a great commercial.

"I think it's fair to say that the franchise owners need to take a step back and let us do our jobs," Steve surmised.

Everyone nodded.

"I also think we need to come up with a creative vision, and then stick with it."

More murmured approval.

"Most importantly, I think this team needs to get its confidence back."

Steve noted several reddened faces. One of the creative consultants looked like he was about to burst into tears. It was hard to imagine a more dysfunctional team than the one arrayed before him.

"I think we have an abundance of talent here," Steve went on. "All we need is greater focus and greater discipline—particularly in how we deal with one another."

The room fell quiet. But Steve was slowly becoming sure of one thing: he was winning these people over. A few minutes later they took a break for lunch and reconvened at 1:00 p.m., whereupon they resumed their analysis of what was wrong with their efforts and how those efforts could be fixed. Steve was further encouraged, as he sensed that he really could learn from these people. Certain key aspects, however, were missing. They needed some reorganization, and they needed someone who could generate "the Brilliant Concept." This team could develop a *sound* concept, and execute it—so long as they had a reasonable budget to work with. They also needed an advocate, someone who could coach them toward success.

Steve saw the latter as his job. This ship could be righted, Steve told himself, and it could be steered with the team he had in place. And that's why he was so shocked by what happened next.

20

A Public Execution

By mid-afternoon the established mood and the conference table was calm. The accusations had stopped, and the adversaries were talking to one another.

As a group they decided to keep the number of large-scale changes to a minimum so that they could more clearly see the correlation between a single change and its effect. They were also going to work on how they interacted with one another. Much to their chagrin, Steve spent the better part of two hours on this one idea which, to them, seemed to have little to do with marketing and advertising Antonio's restaurants in North America. However, Steve was strangely adamant on one point. "You need to trust one another," he insisted. He repeated again and again in various ways, saying they needed to be "invested in one another's success." If they did not succeed as a team, he claimed, they would all fail as individuals. "It's as simple as that," he said. Then, just as Steve was laying out his vision, the door to the conference room unexpectedly swung opened.

To Steve's utter shock, in walked Andreas Zimmerman. Andreas hadn't told Steve he would be attending the meeting. To the contrary, Steve had made a point of telling Andreas that his attendance wasn't necessary.

"Hope I'm not interrupting," Andreas said as he strolled to a chair toward the back of the room.

Steve did his best to conceal his irritation. "That's quite all right," he said.

As Steve spoke, Andreas began to fidget. It seemed to be a deliberate disturbance, one intended to have an unsettling effect. Intuitively, Steve knew that his new boss was not going to approve of all this talk of teamwork. It ran against Andreas's venture capitalist's grain, and Steve could see Andreas taking him to task for all this psychobabble the next time they met in private. But as Steve stood before the group, he reminded himself that he had been put in charge to run this company, and he needed to adhere to the strategies and tactics that had worked for him in the past. Thus, from his discussion of teamwork, Steve tried to move as adroitly as possible to the topic of the franchise owners.

"They're also a part of our team," Steve said, "and we need to listen to what they're telling us."

That's when Andreas did something shocking.

"I've heard what they have to say," he interrupted. "And it isn't a happy message."

The productive atmosphere Steve had worked so hard to establish was now gone. Steve watched on as everyone gazed down at their notes, paralyzed with the fear of what was coming their way.

Turning to Tom, Andreas said, "Have you heard what they have to say?"

"I have," Tom said.

"How would you describe it?"

"I don't know if I can answer that question adequately."

Now Andreas got to his point. "What have you done to introduce new products?" he asked.

"Well, I've …" Tom began.

"Nothing, right?"

"That's not true."

"Then why is it that 830 owners think you're incompetent?"

"Well, we've been working on a strategy this morning that would address …"

"You haven't done anything," Andreas interrupted again, *and that's your fault.*"

"I don't agree with your premise, but you're entitled to …"

Then Andreas shocked the room. "You're fired," he said flatly.

Tom nodded.

"Security will escort you out of the building."

Tom stood. He took a look around the table at his former coworkers, only a few of whom could look him in the eyes. Then he left the room.

Steve suddenly experienced a sharp, penetrating pain that extended from his temple to a very specific point behind his right eye. He also felt a blinding fury. Andreas had completely bypassed his authority in front of the company's entire senior management team. Steve now understood how his new boss motivated his people. It was through fear.

Trying to keep a handle on his anger, Steve calmly called an end to the meeting. As everyone vanished, so did Andreas. The group rose and walked away from the table and out, their eyes wide with shock. They all knew they could be fired at any moment, and that they would be humiliated in front of their peers when it happened. Andreas's statement needed no interpretation.

When Steve returned to his office, his voicemail was lit up like a Christmas tree. Playing back the messages, he took in the harrowing voices of a stunned executive staff, all of which were capped by the furious voice of the HR director. Steve called him immediately.

"This might destroy the company," he explained to Steve in a very blunt conversation. "Several people are talking to me about leaving. These are some of our best people. They're afraid and they're angry."

"We were making some real progress," Steve said. "And then ..."

"People are openly wondering if they want to stay on."

"I'll be meeting with Andreas."

"And there's one more thing. We're now in need of one hell of a marketing chief, and we'll need one right away."

"Let's start looking now."

"I'll put the word out," the HR exec said. "But just answer one question."

"Ask away."

"What caliber of marketing executive would want to work for an outfit that treats its people like this?"

"Excellent point," Steve said. "But you're making it to the wrong person."

21

The Message

Steve was now in a difficult situation, and it was one he could not escape. Everywhere he went the following week his people were stricken with either fear or rage. Meanwhile, Andreas had made himself completely unavailable, escaping by private jet to his home in the Alps immediately after the meeting. He had come in, wreaked his havoc, and left Steve to clean up the mess. A few days later, Zimmerman finally called. His voice was eerily calm.

"I was hoping we could discuss menu options at the top of the week," he said.

"I have a number of matters I'd like to discuss with you as well," Steve said, doing his best to keep his emotions in check.

"Excellent," was Andreas's one-word reply.

◆   ◆   ◆

Steve spent a full half-hour before the meeting rehearsing what he was going to say to Andreas and how he was going to say it. In no uncertain terms he was going to tell him that what he had done was unacceptable. But no matter what happened, Steve resolved to remain calm.

When he finally came into Andreas's office, his boss seemed blissfully unaware of the damage he had inflicted. The incident was barely a memory. His newest business acquisition was no longer functioning, and he had no idea that this was the case or that he was the cause. It even took a few minutes for him to notice that Steve was unusually quiet.

"Is something wrong?" Andreas asked.

"Before we talk about menus," Steve began in a very carefully calibrated tone, "we need to discuss what happened last Friday."

Andreas looked up from a catalogue of recipes he'd received from the company's research kitchen in Hoboken.

"When I fired our marketing director, right?" Andreas said as though puzzled.

"Yes."

"I wanted to be very careful in how I did it," Andreas said. "I did it in just that way to send a message."

"What message were you intending to send?"

"Perform or die," Andreas said with an amused smile.

Andreas studied Steve, clearly trying to discern whether or not he had a problem with this. Steve, however, realized that a moment of truth was at hand.

"That was the message everyone received," he said.

"Excellent."

"But that's not how you get people to perform," he added. "That's how you destroy a company."

"You just said everyone in the room got the message," Andreas replied.

"That's not my point."

"Then *get* to your point."

As intimidated as Steve was at the moment, he was determined not to show it.

"My point is that you sent the *wrong* message," he said.

"What's wrong with that message? I have no doubt that it has inspired everyone to work as though their life depends upon it."

"I'm here to inform you," Steve said, bringing to bear a note of challenge in his voice, "that it hasn't. To the contrary, it has inspired our best people to look elsewhere for work—a place where they can invest themselves in a company that will invest in them. Moreover, it has crippled our ability to recruit great talent. With all due respect, Andreas, word gets around, and nobody wants to work for a company that humiliates its people."

The two let a little silence fall between them. Andreas seemed to be taking the opportunity to size up his audacious new CEO. Steve could only sit and wait in silence to see whether or not he was about to be fired. A moment later, Andreas began nodding.

"I see," he said. "And do you want to keep working for me?"

"Not if my authority is going to be usurped," Steve said.

"You want a free hand to do as you please?"

"I need to be able to support the people I depend upon. If I can't do that, I'll fail. It's as simple as that."

"And who do you depend upon?"

"Every single person who works for Antonio's."

"That's a lot of people to be dependent upon."

"You depend upon them too," Steve said. "You just don't realize it yet."

Andreas appeared to take some offense to the remark. Steve, however, knew in his heart that he wasn't being insolent, and he suspected that Andreas understood this. Steve's realization that he depended upon his subordinates lay at the very center of his past success, and he was not inclined to debate its value or negotiate away the transformative power that lay behind it.

"I should let you run the company as you see fit," Andreas said, breaking the long silence.

"I would appreciate that," Steve replied.

"Of course you will also inherit the responsibility for its performance."

"I would expect that."

"We're going to need a brilliant replacement for Tom."

"And we'll need to fill that position as soon as possible."

"Any leads on promising candidates to fix our marketing department?"

"None whatsoever."

Andreas gave Steve a look of understanding. I get it, he seemed to be saying. "We want someone who can work fast," he said.

"We want the most creative mind we can find," Steve added.

As Steve stood before Andreas and pondered a mental profile of the perfect marketing director, he knew who he wanted for the job. The longer he thought about it, the more convinced he became that there was only one person on the planet capable of turning the company's marketing and advertising around.

"I know exactly who we need," Steve abruptly announced.

"And who is that?" Andreas asked.

"Someone I've known for a very long time."

22

A Dream Team

It didn't take long for Steve to convince Andreas that his old friend Irwin was an inspired choice. His resume spoke for itself. Irwin was the brilliant creative mind they were looking for, the human idea factory that would transform their marketing and advertising in a way that would turn the company around. He was the critical, missing part of the puzzle, everything the hardworking but uninspired Tom had not been. The people they had in place could execute a brilliant strategy as well as they could execute a pathetic one. It was paint-by-numbers, and all they had to do was harness Irwin's energy.

Steve, however, knew that Irwin wasn't going to come cheap—if he was going to come at all. He made a great deal of money where he was, and it would take a sizeable incentive for him to leave the advertising agency that he had helped build into a top-drawer Madison Avenue firm. He'd been their go-to guy for years now, and had brought them nearly $25 million in campaign contracts. They had deep pockets and were not going to just let him go.

"How much does he make?" Andreas asked.

"I have no idea."

"What would you guess?"

"I don't know—$250,000, $500,000? Something like that.

Andreas cleared his throat.

"That's too much," he said.

"All I can tell you is that he's made them a whole lot more," was all Steve could add to that.

Andreas walked around the room, his head bowed in thought.

"The resume isn't enough," Andreas concluded a minute later. "I'll need to look over his entire portfolio."

◆   ◆   ◆

That evening Steve stayed late at the office to scrounge about for the videotapes he had kept of his friend's television commercials. He also found a number of print ads that had run in national magazines. The more Steve found, the more convinced he became of Irwin's genius. Taken together, they were fresh, fun, often funny, and always intriguing. Steve left with nearly a dozen tapes and magazines—more than enough to demonstrate to Andreas that he would be bringing onboard a creative dynamo.

The minute he got home he told Susan what he was up to. Together they went through all of Irwin's work at the dining room table and organized it all chronologically. An invigorating excitement took over as they worked at the kitchen table. Susan was thrilled by the possibility of the two of them working together. But she too was doubtful that Irwin would leave his firm.

"It's a long shot," Steve said.

"But if it happens, you guys will be unstoppable."

"We're opposites."

"You're complementary," his wife remarked. "Two halves of a whole."

This was precisely what Steve found so alluring about the prospect. Irwin, he knew, was his professional alter ego.

The effort immediately gained momentum when, at the top of the following week, Steve received a memo from Andreas stating that he'd reviewed the tapes, and that he wanted Irwin on board ASAP. Attached to the memo was an outline of a financial package that Steve could not quite fathom. He knew that Irwin made a lot of money at the ad firm. But this was a whole new level of compensation.

Steve waited until Irwin was home from work before he called with the news. Irwin couldn't quite get his mind around what he was hearing.

"He's offering *what?*" Irwin asked.

Steve repeated the numbers. "It's an offer you can't refuse," he added.

"Steve," Irwin said, "I can't leave the agency. I helped build it."

"But you're our man," Steve said. "I'm sure of it. As you can see for yourself, Zimmerman is sure of it too."

"He has certainly made himself clear," Irwin mumbled. "But I'd have to think it over. It would be a *huge* move …"

"Then think it over," Steve said. "And then call me tomorrow to give me your start date."

"It won't be tomorrow," was all Irwin could say to that.

◆   ◆   ◆

Although it was something of a pipe dream, Steve knew that if he and Irwin were working together, they could turn this franchise business into the centerpiece of the Zimmerman Empire. After five years, the company would be worth several times what Andreas had paid for it, and Steve would be garnering 30% of the gain. Irwin himself would be nearly as well compensated. But the dream extended beyond money in Steve's mind. He pictured this being one of those legendary corporate turn-around stories that people would talk about for decades to come. This was the Chrysler story in the making; this was Kimberly-Clark, Gillette, GE. Steve would be able to retire at forty-five. He and Susan would walk off into the sunset together … and yet he couldn't imagine accomplishing any of this without Irwin's help. Nor could he imagine Irwin giving up the job that had served so well as the stage for his remarkable talents for so long.

And that's why it was such a surprise when the following Monday Steve received a message on his answering machine. It was a voice that did not identify itself. It simply said, "I'm in."

The voice, he knew, was Irwin's.

23

The Inspired Choice

The excitement was electric around the restaurant table that night. Surrounded by their families, the two friends shared ideas about how they were going to execute new branding for Antonio's.

To Steve's delight, Irwin began spinning off advertising campaigns, complete with strategy and tactics, one right after another, right there at the table. Some were simple and elegant, others sophisticated and beautiful. They would use every arrow in Irwin's quiver, while Steve was going to assemble a team so dedicated to this mission, so motivated and so cohesive that Irwin was going to think he had died and gone to ad-man heaven. As the chatter extended deep into the night, Steve felt an excitement that he had never known in his professional life. This was going to work. Indeed, there was no way it was going to fail. And it was going to work in a very big way.

◆   ◆   ◆

There were two central reasons why Irwin took the job. The most obvious was the money. Simply put, the job came with lots of it. The second reason, however, was the deal maker, because it made all the difference to Irwin: He'd always harbored a deep admiration for Steve. Most significantly, he admired Steve for the risks he had consistently taken throughout his career.

While Irwin had quietly watched on in amazement, Steve had gone out on a very long limb in not authorizing the bribe to corrupt customs officials in the Caribbean all those years ago. Then he had gone out on an even longer limb in backing the TTM satellite technology. Had either risk failed, Steve's career would have been mortally wounded. Steve then cut in an entirely new direction when he decided to head up the decrepit Gunther Company. He breathed life into a factory that, by now, would be boarded up, its employees let go, the building bulldozed and the lot turned into storage units. And now here he was at the right hand of Andreas Zimmerman, poised to turn his most impressive hat trick yet—and with Irwin's help. Opportunities like this were exceedingly rare. There was no way Irwin was going to simply pass on it in favor of doing what he had been doing day-in and day-out for the past fifteen years.

What piqued Irwin's professional interest in Steve was something that had always puzzled him. Irwin had no idea what the secret to Steve's success was. Granted, Steve was a brilliant accountant. But Irwin knew dozens of brilliant accountants, none of whom could approach Steve's success. Steve also had sound business instincts. He had, after all, picked the satellite concept, and had seen the latent potential in the Gunther Company. In this latter example, however, he had had to realize that potential himself. He made it happen by sheer force of will, and that kind of power in such an unassuming person intrigued Irwin. But how, exactly, had Steve actually accomplished it? Irwin had never worked with Steve, so he had no idea. But he definitely wanted to find out.

Irwin also had ambitions of his own that he openly wanted to advance. Steve had intimated to him that he would be a likely candidate for succeeding him should the new buyer be seeking an in-house replacement for him as CEO. Of course Irwin would have to perform. After analyzing the clunky marketing and advertising work the company had produced under the auspices of his predecessor, Irwin was sure he would be received as a miracle worker. But there was one big catch. The advertising concepts Irwin wanted to employ were going to cost a small fortune. He was going to have to convince Steve—and of course Zimmerman—that the returns they would see on these campaigns would be well worth it, that it made good business sense. Whether Zimmerman knew it or not, he was going to be writing another batch of very big checks.

Over the course of the next week, Irwin began putting together a preliminary marketing and advertising plan that included a detailed budget. The plan's centerpiece was an elaborate, well-coordinated television and radio campaign that would effectively re-brand Antonio's as an up-market family restaurant. Re-branding, they had agreed, was the heart and soul of the transformation they were looking to bring about. But there were costs inherent to such an ambitious project, costs that went far beyond the campaigns themselves. As Irwin put the numbers together, he saw that it was going to be much more expensive for the franchisees than even *he* had initially thought.

This would make the entire endeavor politically complicated. To re-brand meant it would inevitably fall to the 830 franchise owners to cough up money for new kitchen equipment, such as gas grills, and decorative upgrades, such as Italianate tile and mood-inducing sconce lighting in their restaurants. Irwin had already heard colorful stories of their discontent with the corporate office, and doubted they were going to accept the proposal that Irwin was going to put before them. Zimmerman certainly wasn't going to offer to pay for any of it, and so there was no alternative. The company's transformation from lousy to great was going to be measured in dollars. That was business. No one should have to explain any of this to Andreas Zimmerman.

But Irwin was confident in his plan. He'd been in the business long enough to recognize a consistent pattern with clients, employers and general managers. They always began as skeptics, especially when it came time to write the big check. And then slowly but inevitably their opinion began to evolve. Finally, when the revenues came pouring in six months later, they were Irwin's best friend. They suddenly forgot about their annoying objections to his creative choices, and only recalled having stood by him all along. It was a frustration that came with his job, one Irwin had learned to endure with equanimity. But this time things were a little different. This time he was working for Steve, someone who didn't fit the mold of the conventional businessman.

Once Irwin had finished his proposal he took it to his friend. He sat before Steve's cluttered desk and watched on as he registered sticker shock.

"This is one expensive plan," Steve said.

"But it will work," Irwin replied. "And, as history has taught us, going cheap will not."

"Who's going to pay for it?"

"The people who will benefit the most."

"The franchisees."

"The trick is convincing them that they will benefit."

"If you asked them to vote on it today," Steve said with a note of concern in his voice, "not a single owner would vote in favor. I'd guarantee it."

Steve then began pounding out numbers on the calculator with Irwin sitting next to him. A minute later Steve turned the calculator to Irwin. He concluded that it would require franchisees to accept an increase of approximately 2% of their gross annual revenues, just to be playing in the same league as other successful restaurant chains.

"I don't think that's out of line," Irwin said.

"You obviously have faith in this approach."

"It will change everything."

"So it's just a matter of changing minds."

Steve drummed his fingers as he gazed up at the ceiling tiles.

"We need to show them what this approach will do," Steve said. "We need to show them that it's going to take the entire chain to a whole new level, and that the profits will far outweigh the costs."

"It will redefine Antonio's in the mind of the American consumer," Irwin added.

"And it's going to be great."

His old friend, Irwin realized, was unconventional indeed.

24

Swinging for the Fences

Irwin's proposal met with a very different reception from Zimmerman. As Steve expected, he was not only put-off but actually angered by the extraordinary expense.

"This is a nonstarter," he nearly shouted at Steve and Irwin. "You don't just spend your way into profits."

"The brand needs to be reinvented," Steve countered. "This isn't just a campaign, but a whole new strategy for a whole new kind of restaurant."

"We already have a brand!"

"We have a tired brand," Irwin interjected. "And it's not producing results."

"Irwin has succeeded with this kind of strategy before," Steve chimed in.

The room was silent as Steve and Irwin waited for Zimmerman to respond.

"Somebody would have to convince the franchisees," he finally grumbled under his breath. "Frankly, I don't think that's possible."

"I think I can do it if I show them a business plan with a fatter bottom line," Steve said.

Andreas cast Steve a look over the top of his architect's glasses. It was a look of ridicule. Steve had drunk his own Kool-Aid and now thought he could convince anyone of anything with a folksy conversation.

"Do you realize how upset they are with us right now?" Andreas asked.

"I know exactly how upset," Steve said.

Andreas shook his head.

"This approach is fundamentally different from what I had envisioned," Andreas plaintively moaned. "It's … too broad in scope … too grandiose … I just wanted to buy a company, spank it into shape, and flip it. That's all. None of this … *re-branding* …"

◆   ◆   ◆

Once again, Steve took to the road, crisscrossing the country in his campaign to convince his disgruntled franchisees that they should spend 2% of their gross annual revenues to update their shabby little restaurants. He held out no illusions. Nevertheless, he immediately came to detect a general sense of goodwill from a solid majority of the owners when he first introduced himself, a gratitude for having taken the time to go out into the field and see things from their point of view. He genuinely felt it was a starting point for a new working relationship.

And yet, the initial reception he received at each of his stops was everything he had expected. A 72-year-old owner in Cedar Rapids, Iowa shouted, "You come in here asking for 2% of my money so that you can make a fool of me on national TV?" The response was representative of how nearly all of the conversations began. Steve was a nice, fresh face from the corporate office, but there was no way on God's green earth that he was going to submit to any such scheme.

But each meeting had a predictable arc. At some point in nearly every conversation Steve sensed an opening, a moment in which the owner realized that he had come all this way, and that they owed it to him to at least give his proposal serious thought. And that's when Steve made his move. Out came the charts, out came the spreadsheets.

"We either grow or we die," Steve always began. "And we're looking to drive business to a whole new level."

Within twenty minutes, the elderly Cedar Rapids owner was grudgingly won over. And so nearly all of them were.

As Steve moved from store to store, he convinced each owner that he saw him or her as a partner. They were all in this together and they depended upon one another to succeed. It was a surprisingly easy sell to make because it was true. Listening to the owners had a calming effect on them. He knew how to talk honestly about what they were afraid of, what their hopes were, what they were angry about. The face-to-face discussions also let them get a glimpse of the bigger picture—his picture, the picture from headquarters—of how things could change and become better for everyone. That was, after all, the essence of the franchise business model, and this was how he was able to envision the company bringing about an extraordinary result. As he moved from city to city, restaurant to restaurant, Steve slowly convinced a solid majority of owners of one simple fact: the way forward, the way to greater profits, was through mutual investment.

25

Conflict

On Steve's first day back, he was greeted by four senior marketing people milling around outside his office door.

"We need to talk," Margaret, his senior marketing coordinator said as he approached. The other three stood behind her with a look of alarm in their eyes.

"Come on in," he said.

They all filed past, with the last closing the door behind him. Steve leaned against the front edge of his desk and asked what the matter was.

"Irwin," Margaret said.

Steve shook his head. "I've been on the road for the past two weeks. You'll have to be more specific."

The five exchanged a look, and then Margaret began.

The story Steve listened to over the next hour caught him off balance. He'd never heard of anything like it. Irwin, he was told, was not so much an idea man, but an idea factory. He had far too many, which he rattled off, one right after another, without any rhyme or rhythm. One minute, he was demanding new menus, the next a new product, and ten minutes later he was shouting that they needed to buy more television time in one market and cancel it in another. As he spat out each idea, he expected the people around him to make it happen—immediately.

"It's a mess," the advertising coordinator claimed. "The orders conflict with one another, nothing's thought out … it's just one idea piled on top of another."

"We have no way of implementing any of it," she said, "so nothing's getting done."

"I see," Steve said.

"Don't get me wrong," she added. "Irwin's brilliant. I mean, he comes up with a hundred concepts a day. No one's ever seen anything like it."

"We have no way of knowing what needs to be done first, what should wait," Michael, the electronic media coordinator added.

"We're stuck," Margaret said, tears welling up in her eyes. "Really stuck."

The meeting ended with Steve promising to approach Irwin about the problem immediately. They smiled skeptically.

Once they were gone, Steve considered how difficult it must be to work for someone like Irwin. The more he thought about it, the more their complaints rang true. While Irwin was great at generating ideas, he didn't necessarily have the temperament or discipline to marshal them and shape them into great content. Nor was Irwin naturally given to working as the leader of a team. It was a critical shortcoming, Steve realized, one that he would personally have to address. He would need some coaching if he was going to succeed here.

26

Merely Competent

Before approaching Irwin, Steve wanted to develop a clear picture of his friend's critics. After checking some files and asking a few subtle questions of the people in his department, he got one.

Michael and Lewis were British advertising veterans who had worked together for more than a decade in London before coming to New York City. While they had solid reputations for competence, they were not the most creative duo in the world. Nevertheless, they executed reasonably well. James was a sartorially dressed, mild-mannered forty-two-year-old Clemson graduate who took his job home with him every night. He wasn't one to engage in turf wars or drum up conflict for his own purposes. Then again, neither were the Brits. Margaret, the senior marketing coordinator who had led the charge against Irwin, was the wild card. Steve simply did not know what to make of her.

With her ankle-length skirts, unsmiling demeanor, and salt-and-pepper hair which she kept bailed up with long steel pins, she reminded Steve of an English classics professor he'd had back at NYU. Margaret in fact came from an academic background, holding an MBA and MFA from Cornell. But her post as senior marketing coordinator for a national restaurant chain seemed an unlikely career choice. She looked like she'd be more at home in academia rather than the corporate world. And yet she was very good at what she did. She worked incredibly hard and was exceedingly organized—some said to a fault. Everything had to be kept running according to her flow charts, or she became unhinged and let her displeasure be known to everyone within earshot. In any event, she kept the trains running on time, and Steve didn't want to loose her.

On a personal level, Margaret simply wasn't warm. Steve noticed that people often kept their distance, even those who had worked closely with her for years. And yet she had her allies, all of whom seemed unusually devoted to her. Steve didn't know what her opinion of Irwin was beyond what she had said, but he could only guess that it wasn't positive. He could only assume that her problems with Irwin were based in reality, and that they were only going to get worse unless something was done. The trick, he knew, was to make Irwin aware of the problem without alienating him.

◆　　　◆　　　◆

The following afternoon Steve went into Irwin's office bearing the good news of his trip.

"I think they see the light," he said. "The owners will be voting on the allocation later this week."

Irwin clapped his hands.

"So, how did you manage that?" he said, thoroughly and amazed.

"You start off shooting the breeze with these people," Steve went on. "And then you make your pitch. When that doesn't work, you reason with them. Out comes the calculator, out come the charts. You learn from them, they learn from you."

Irwin nodded. Once again, Steve's trusted M.O. had yielded results. "So we can begin buying air time," Irwin said.

"We need to address a few other matters before we move ahead."

Irwin sat up.

"I want to know exactly how we're going to proceed," Steve went on. "Most importantly, I want the advertising and marketing departments working together as a team."

Irwin gave Steve a quizzical look.

"What are you getting at?" he asked.

"I'm going to schedule a meeting," Steve said. "I want all of the principal elements of advertising and marketing there. I want everyone to be able to speak freely and openly."

"Is there a problem?" Irwin asked.

Steve paused and thought for a moment.

"You're brilliant," he said. "In fact, you're the brightest person I've ever known. But your brilliance causes you to be a little ..."

"Overwhelming."

Steve nodded. "Let's schedule the meeting for the weekend," he said. "We'll go over everything then."

Irwin pushed himself away from the desk.

"Steve, I've got a thousand—maybe two-thousand—things that are more pressing than fostering teamwork."

Steve shook his head. Irwin was his closest friend, and he knew he could be direct.

"Trust me," he said as he moved for the door. "Nothing's more important than this meeting."

◆   ◆   ◆

The more Steve thought about it, the more convinced he became of the meeting's significance. Ultimately he decided to make it an off-site retreat, as this would allow everyone to focus on one all-important concept. Their success depended upon whether or not they could come together to form a cohesive unit. Steve didn't want to be overly dramatic in making the point, but it would be best to begin this Herculean undertaking with this one idea squarely in the minds of everyone around him.

A few years back, Steve and Susan had spent a long weekend at an inn on the outskirts of Cornwall, New York, a small town overlooking the Hudson River Valley. The inn was large enough to host ten or twelve people and yet small enough to lend the impression that they were "away," removed from the noise and pressures of the workaday world. If he recalled correctly, the man even had a large dining room with an enormous dinner table set before a huge fireplace. It would be perfect for a company a retreat.

The inn was a two-hour drive north out of the city, and, as it turned out, it was available. Steve made the reservation on the spot, and then called around to Irwin and each of the functional leaders in advertising and marketing to tell them what they would be doing this weekend. When asked what the meeting was about, Steve explained: "We need to develop this team's ability to communicate before we start implementing the large-scale changes we have planned."

"You don't think we can do that here at the office?" Irwin asked. "We see each other every day."

"It's important that we do something out of the ordinary to build this team," was all Steve would say.

"You're the boss."

Only the chief television consultant protested. He and his wife, he argued, had an appointment with a real estate agent, so he wouldn't be able to make it.

"The meeting is mandatory," he said. "Everyone needs to be there."

"I already know everyone," the consultant said, "and they already know me."

"It will only be successful if everyone participates," Steve said with an unmistakable note of certainty, "and you need to be there."

The fact that Steve had placed so much emphasis on the retreat alarmed nearly everyone. It had even given Irwin pause. What was a little gathering at a bed-and-breakfast on the Hudson River going to do for them or the company? How was it going to fundamentally change the dynamics of what they were up against in transforming a national restaurant chain? Even Margaret and the marketing people who had approached Steve with their concerns thought the move to be a gross over-reaction. All they had wanted was for Irwin to organize his approach to the overall marketing and advertising strategy. Steve and Irwin could discuss the matter over lunch; this was what disconcerted them about Steve's announcement. Their new CEO, it seemed, did not know how to calibrate his response to delicate matters. And he was so *sure* of what he was doing.

"Announcing a retreat over the matter," Margaret told her assistant, "is like swatting a fly with a shovel.

27

Vulnerabilities

It was a brilliant autumn day, the colors of upstate New York just beginning to turn. Steve took the exquisite weather and vibrant colors as a good omen. The ten members of the marketing and advertising teams drove up from the city and arrived early. Everyone, that is, except Irwin.

The itinerary called for the group to gather on the vast wrap-around front porch of the bed-and-breakfast at noon. They checked in, marveled at the quaint setting, and carried their bags up the broad staircase to their rooms. Once they had a chance to settle in, they came out to the porch and stood in amazement of the view of the Hudson River Valley. Seeing this, Steve felt renewed confidence in his larger plan. He had set a very low threshold of success for the weekend. What he wanted to accomplish was simple: for his people to spend time together in the hopes of building relationships that would serve as a platform for open communication with one another. Once they had let their guard down, they might begin to look at themselves as part of something bigger. Not until that was accomplished could they even begin to attempt something as complex as prioritizing collective goals and developing strategy. First things had to come first. A deep breath was in order. Everyone would come to the meeting casually dressed; suits and ties were forbidden.

With the exception of Irwin's tardiness, all was going just as Steve had hoped. Scattered groups milled about and visited on the lawn, or sat on the steps. Steve noted, however, that they tended to visit those coworkers within their own tribe. It was like a high school sock hop, where each person was part of a clique. There was nothing cruel about the groups. Every now and then Steve overheard someone casually talking shop, but for the most part they were sharing stories of their children, their spouses, city life, or just marveling at the spectacular view.

By 1:00 p.m., however, Irwin still hadn't arrived. Steve felt a mounting anxiety as he stood on the front porch waiting for the hum of Irwin's BMW. A distressing thought gradually emerged. What if Irwin didn't show up? Or what if he showed up late? Steve had been so adamant with everyone about attending this retreat over their weekend. It would appear as though he had inverted double standards—a much higher one for those further down in the pecking order, and one much lower for those further up. Everybody had scratched weekend plans with their families so that they could attend. Irwin, apparently, had not.

Time passed, and Irwin was still a no-show. Finally, by two o'clock Steve decided it was time to call everyone in around the dining room table. As awkward as this would be without Irwin, it was all Steve could do. And it was at that final moment, just as Steve was about to raise his voice, that he saw the glint of a sports car racing up the switchbacks.

Steve continued to make small talk in order to allow Irwin time to make his arrival appear on schedule. Everyone was deeply immersed in their conversations, everyone content to be away from the city. Steve was thanked repeatedly for having invited them. As he shot the breeze with Margaret, he saw Irwin walking up to him looking a little harried. He shook Steve's and Margaret's hands, and then congratulated Steve on his taste in views.

"This is stunning," he said.

"Have trouble getting out of the city?" Steve said.

Irwin rolled his eyes.

"I was in the office this morning and got carried away," Irwin said. "When I get started on something good, I lose all track of time."

Margaret cocked her head to one side and said, "I think you have too many ideas."

"That's my job," Irwin said with a shrug. "I'm the company Idea Man."

Margaret nodded skeptically, not entirely convinced of Irwin's worthiness of the title.

"Anyway," Irwin went on, "it gave me a chance to storyboard some spots that I think everyone's going to love. Even you, Margaret."

Margaret smiled but said nothing. Steve, on the other hand, was saying to himself: This is Irwin all over again. You think he's going to fail you when, at the very last moment, he delivers everything you asked for, and then some. He shows up late, but with a bushel basket of million-dollar ideas.

The group kept up the chatter as they sat around the sprawling antique oak table under antler candelabra. To Steve's mind, the moment could not have been more auspicious. The tribalism seemed to be melting away. Someone told a joke, which inspired Margaret, who wasn't known for her sense of humor, to tell another that buckled the group over with laughter. Margaret appeared moved by the reaction she got. Then Irwin delivered a joke with a couple of well-placed four-letter words that left several people in fits of uncontrolled laughter. As Steve sat back, observing it all, he was convinced that these people genuinely liked one another. No one was pretending to be having fun. It reasoned that the problem Irwin was having with his staff was a matter of organization and execution, not some deep-running conflict of personality. The remedy therefore was relatively straight-forward: get everyone to see that they needed to work in concert with one another. Once that was accomplished, they could then hone a method for carrying out Irwin's vision.

The moment Steve opened the meeting the room fell quiet and the atmosphere unexpectedly became serious.

"I invited everyone up here this weekend for a reason," he said as he strode before the marble fireplace. "It's to convince you all of one thing. This single concept trumps all other aspects of what we do. I would even go so far as to say that without it everything we do is bound to fail."

Steve saw that a couple of his people were taking notes. Seeing this, he stopped in mid-sentence, and said, "This isn't something you'll have to write down. This is about commitment. What I want to establish this weekend is our commitment to one another's success. If we don't succeed as a team, we will fail as a company. It's as simple as that."

Steve carefully studied the reactions of everyone at the table. Some appeared to reject the idea outright, and wouldn't bother to pretend that they thought it worthy of their attention. Most had no reaction whatsoever. The point left this latter group visibly under-whelmed. The weekend might turn out to be a two-day pep talk after all.

So Steve moved on to specifics.

"I want to take a minute and have everyone write down what they're afraid of," he said.

With this, a few of the people rolled their eyes as though fearing some unendurable anguish was coming their way. Irwin sat stock-still. He looked downright alarmed.

Steve made a gesture toward the tablets lying before each of them. No one could quite believe it. They were actually being asked to *scrawl down their fears on paper*, fears that, apparently, they were going to have to *share with their coworkers*. Would they be fired if they were too direct and honest? Would they be allowed to admit that they were afraid of being humiliated before everyone at the table? They were being asked to reveal their vulnerabilities to people whom they did not necessarily trust.

"Go ahead," Steve said. "Tell everyone that you're afraid the new boss is going to drive the business into the ground. Tell everyone here that you're afraid of being fired by Andreas Zimmerman in front of your friends. You can say anything you want. Nothing is off limits."

Still, no one was ready to take Steve up on his offer. At least not right away. It took a few minutes for the first person to jot down a three-word fragment. Once this small precedent had been established, however, the rest gradually followed suit with a smattering of words, or a sentence or two. Some actually took the opportunity to write at length. Margaret was one of these people. The opportunity to write it all down seemed to be a catharsis for her. Ten minutes into the project the last of the scrawling had stopped, and Steve asked Margaret to begin.

"My greatest fear is simple," she said. "It's that we'll fail in the next few weeks and months, and then the business we're trying so hard to build will completely collapse."

There was a moment of dead silence.

And then, quite unexpectedly, the table erupted in laughter. Margaret was visibly taken aback. She looked as though she had been betrayed, and turned her gaze to Steve in an appeal for help. Wasn't she and everyone else supposed to be able to write anything they wanted with impunity? This wasn't exactly fair. And then slowly—very slowly at first—Margaret realized just how unbuckled she must have sounded, and she broke a faint smile.

"It could happen," Irwin said as the laughter subsided.

"I suppose that's my greatest fear too," Steve added.

Once the room quieted, he proceeded around the table, with some of the people giving personal answers to the question.

"I'm afraid that I'll devote a huge amount of time and work to a project that everyone ends up hating," the art director admitted.

"My biggest fear is that I'll make one small mistake that will end up dragging down an entire project," the head of marketing collateral offered.

A few others could only come up with "Ditto," or "You're singing my song." These cop outs, however, were more than compensated for by Margaret when she announced that she had a second fear. Famous for her direct, no-nonsense, manner, Steve noticed those around her cringing in anticipation of what she was about to say.

"I fear," she began, "that we've become paralyzed."

So the big moment was at hand. Steve knew exactly where she was going with this, as did everyone else. Irwin rotated ninety degrees in his seat so that Margaret could address him directly. He didn't appear offended. To the contrary, he looked prepared—even grateful—to have grievances aired directly at him instead of behind his back. And that was exactly what Margaret was about to do.

"You believe we've become paralyzed as a team?" Steve asked.

"As a team," she said, "as a group of individuals—whatever you want to call us. We're paralyzed because we don't have any direction, and we don't have any priorities. All we have is a flurry of orders coming down from above." She paused, looked around the table, and then added, "Everyone here knows this is the case."

Steve was taken aback by Margaret's blunt approach. Nevertheless, he thought it best not to show it; she was doing exactly what Steve had told everyone they could do. It was at this point that Irwin broke in. What he said startled everyone at the table.

"Let's get everything out in the open, Margaret" he said. "We all know you're talking about me."

"Who else would I be talking about?" she said as though exasperated.

"Let me just say that this isn't the first time I've heard this criticism," Irwin replied.

Irwin's admission left Steve slightly amazed. How had he been so successful in the past if he really was as disorganized as Margaret suggested he was?

"You have to be more linear with us," she said in a raised voice. "We're *overwhelmed* ..."

"I can be overwhelming," Irwin agreed. "I admit as much. I'm an advertising guy. I get paid to generate ideas."

"You need to generate priorities," she pressed, "not just ideas. We need a strategy that we can methodically pursue. We don't need one idea after another after another!"

"Okay, Margaret, I get it. Priorities, strategy. Less emphasis on ideas."

At this point Steve took the opportunity to come to Irwin's defense.

"Ideas are your brilliance," he interjected.

"We can all agree on that," Margaret said.

"But it's also your Achilles' heel," Steve added.

"Agreed," Irwin said. "What more can I say?"

28

Hard-earned Trust

Exasperation was gradually replaced by a growing sense of cohesion as the weekend advanced. It dawned on people what Steve was up to. He had taken everyone out of the office and into the countryside where tempers had been allowed to flare. Grievances could be aired and addressed, and now, after two short days, they knew one another in a way they hadn't until now.

Nearly everyone had worked in this office for several years now, and yet this was the first time any of them had felt connected to the office as a whole. Irwin and Margaret were not going to become best friends, but they had come to understand one another in a way that neither one of them would have allowed before. Their conflict would have escalated, growing more and more corrosive as time went on, while the team became less and less effective. But instead, Irwin now felt that Margaret, for all of her ungoverned anger and anxiety, wanted things to move in the same direction. They didn't need to like one another, but now they at least saw one another as deserving of respect.

Steve was pleased. He thought he could reduce their working relationship down to three declarative statements: 1.) Irwin and Margaret have very little in common; 2.) Irwin and Margaret have very different talents and very different personalities; 3.) So long as Irwin and Margaret are not in conflict, their differences are good for business.

◆   ◆   ◆

Six months into the job, Steve believed that he and Irwin were finally prepared to begin making critical decisions. To that end, Irwin developed an integrated advertising and marketing strategy that Margaret's team could begin executing. Irwin had brought in a new television production agency, and redirected what he explained to Steve as "the positioning of the brand to the consumer." In the previous quarter the franchise owners had initiated and carried out most of the remodeling of the restaurants, along with a retooling of the menus. The test kitchen in New Jersey had developed a number of dishes that a prominent New York food critic announced in the *Post* as being "abundantly flavorful." The menu selections, he claimed, were "tantalizing." Zimmerman was pleased but skeptical of how much business a single review would generate.

Meanwhile, Irwin pressed Steve to buy more targeted ratings points in the television and radio markets where large clusters of their restaurants were located. They would begin airing a new series of commercials that were catchy and sumptuously produced. Above all, the spots were memorable, and yet Zimmerman criticized them for being "abundantly expensive." In any case, the apparatus they had put in place was set to swing into action the moment Irwin decided that it was time to pull the trigger. But no one knew whether or not the enormous investment in this astonishingly elaborate strategy would work. Even Irwin seemed to be hedging his bets.

"It might produce results," he morosely said, "it might not. You just never know with these things."

Steve found Irwin's sudden caginess troubling. Was this his usual anxiety talking, or did Irwin know something Steve did not? Whichever the case, Steve suddenly realized that his own job was on the line. If this effort failed, Zimmerman would fire him in front of his subordinates, and then security would escort him out of the building like a criminal. Once again, Steve was all set up to be either the hero or the villain in an unfolding business drama of his own making.

The trigger was finally pulled in the spring. Irwin had suggested waiting for the changing of the seasons, as his market research indicated this was the time of year when people were once again leaving the house after a long, cold winter. Moreover, they were more willing to try new things. After being inundated by Irwin's television and radio commercials, the hope was that the American public would be curious to find out what the fuss was all about.

The initial results were not encouraging. Register receipts actually dipped in the Northeast and the Midwest. This was compensated for on the West Coast and the South, where receipts saw a slight up-tick. By the end of the first week, Steve began to make plans for every contingency. All the while he decided to keep the news from Susan simply because he had no idea how to broach the subject. Impending failure meant a catastrophic life change for his wife and daughter, a thought he could hardly allow himself to contemplate.

At the top of the second week, the numbers actually improved a little, but not enough to satisfy Zimmerman. Andreas called Steve and said in a very direct voice, "This does not look good."

"The campaign hasn't run its course," Steve countered.

But Steve had no idea whether or not his boss heard him. Zimmerman, he realized, had hung up on him in mid-sentence.

In any event, there was little Steve could do but sit back and watch the anemic register receipts while Irwin set to work on a new round of advertising. And that's when the other shoe fell. Two weeks into the effort, Steve received a voice message from Zimmerman. He and Irwin were being invited to attend an "emergency conference" at 4:00 p.m. the following Friday. "Your attendance," Zimmerman explained in his faint accent, "is mandatory."

So that's it, Steve said to himself. After hanging up, he called Irwin.

"I got the same call ten minutes ago," he said. "We just need a little more time. It's still early."

"Well, I'm calling to tell you that we've just run out of time."

"The weather is clearing across the country. That alone could change things."

"It's over."

"Not yet."

Three nights later, the night before Steve fully expected to be fired, he received a call from Irwin who was still at the office.

"It isn't over," he said cryptically.

"What's happening?" Steve asked.

"Accounting just called," he said. "The numbers spiked yesterday. We're on a tear on both coasts, the Midwest, the South—everywhere."

Steve had to take a moment to discern whether or not he was dreaming.

The numbers, however, were very real.

◆   ◆   ◆

When Steve and Irwin stepped into the conference room the following afternoon, they were met with a round of applause. Margaret was the first to congratulate Irwin on his "brilliant strategy." Then she approached Steve. "You've worked a miracle," she said. Then, with a somber look in her eyes, she added, "But it might be too late."

Margaret turned away and took her seat, and then everyone quietly awaited the arrival of the man who had called this meeting. Zimmerman, however, was a no-show ten minutes after the meeting was scheduled to begin, a fact not lost on this group of executives who knew the habits of Andreas Zimmerman. He wasn't one to be late for anything and was known for firing those who were. While everyone visited, they exchanged looks of utter shock. Could you believe this? Something, everyone quietly agreed, was up.

As the minutes passed, Irwin and Steve grew more anxious. Finally Steve turned to his friend.

"Zimmerman's arranging our security escort," he whispered.

"That's why he's late," Irwin said.

"You're sure there's nothing wrong with the numbers?"

"You're the accountant."

A full half hour after the meeting was scheduled to begin, Zimmerman burst through the door in a flourish. His hair, which he always kept sleek and heavily pomaded, was mussed. His $3,000 suit looked like he'd slept in it the night before. Andreas Zimmerman was out of sorts. Then it occurred to Steve why Andreas was late. He had been waiting to get the latest telemetry numbers from the Newark office to be sure they were accurate. He had been waiting to see whether or not he would be firing the pair. And now the two old friends were about to discover their fates.

"I have some news," Zimmerman said. "The latest register receipts have come in.

Zimmerman paused. It seemed he wanted Steve and Irwin to endure as much anguish as he could possibly deliver.

"What do they indicate?" Steve finally had to ask.

"They indicate that the latest marketing campaign has not been a complete fiasco."

Steve turned to Irwin who was silently fuming.

"In fact, it looks like we're going to go ahead and purchase more air time in certain markets," Zimmerman added. "Perhaps the recent foul weather on the East Coast played a factor here ... I don't know ..."

And then Zimmerman turned and left the room as abruptly as he had entered thirty seconds earlier.

Once he was gone, Irwin caught Steve's eye. Irwin had his hands on the crown of his head, and made a picture of utter disbelief.

Against all odds, they were still alive.

29

A Commuted Sentence

Early Sunday morning Steve and Irwin arrived at the office at the same time to deal with odds and ends. Except for the janitors, the place was empty. Irwin flopped down on a chair before Steve's desk, kicked his feet up, and began laughing.

"We were standing blindfolded in the courtyard," he murmured, "when our sentences were commuted."

"So what was it?" Steve asked. "What turned the numbers around?"

"Weather, market penetration," Irwin said. "Probably a combination of the two. It just took a week or two longer for people to decide that they wanted to eat somewhere new for a change. That's just the way marketing is, and nobody can tell you why."

Steve shook his head.

"I have to tell you," Steve said. "I didn't know what I was going to tell Susan if we were fired."

"Sheila would have been hearing the same news," Irwin said. He shivered involuntarily, trying to shake off the overwhelming horror of what might have been.

There was a long moment of silence as they sat there. Finally, Irwin sat up and said, "So what's the plan going forward?"

"I don't know," Steve said. "But I have to admit that I don't have the warm-fuzzies for Zimmerman right now."

"I have one suggestion."

"What's that?"

"Let's keep him out of our work from here on."

"How do we do that?"

Irwin sat in silence. He seemed to be giving the idea serious consideration.

"Just ignore him," Irwin said.

"We can't ignore him," Steve said. "He's the boss."

◆   ◆   ◆

Contrary to expectations, the revenue spike held its own through the summer and well into the fall. The overwhelming majority of franchise owners were pleased, and especially pleased with Steve. He was their man. They had placed their trust with this small, unassuming guy who'd gone out of his way to meet them and to see the franchise business from their point of view. And now their trust was paying a healthy dividend. It was this mutual trust, which certain owners spoke of as a "friendship," that provided for a new level of cooperation where before there had been conflict. Headquarters and owners were no longer fighting. Instead, that energy was now being channeled and harnessed, and important work getting done.

But Zimmerman was mystified by Steve's general modus operandi. And he wasn't fond of mysteries.

"I don't see how your approach works," he said in a moment of candor with Steve. "It seems to me to be little more than making friends with the people you work with."

"There's more to it than that," Steve replied. "But that's the heart and soul of it."

"So what am I paying you to do?"

"You're paying me to make this company of restaurants, which are scattered all across North America, to work as one large, efficient and profitable team."

Steve could see that Zimmerman didn't particularly like his answer. After a long, thoughtful silence, Andreas replied: "That's too simple."

Steve could only shrug.

The revenues were not overwhelming, but they were, as Zimmerman himself characterized them to the staff, "substantial." The campaign's most impressive measure of success was its stamina. As winter approached, the numbers remained strong. Flush with cash, Zimmerman once again approved more funding for another round of television and radio spots that would air just as the original commercials were going stale. Unfortunately, there was a significant lag.

By January business began to ratchet down, and then it began to fall off rather abruptly. The profits began to diminish as one advertising issue after another erupted. In no time at all Irwin found himself in the crosshairs of angry owners, and of course Zimmerman. One morning, Andreas laid into him for a solid hour, constantly referring to Irwin as his "marketing Einstein" who "couldn't sell tea in

China." How could he have just let the advertising languish like this when there obviously needed to be strong follow-up?

Painful as it was, Steve stepped into the breach and, in a company-wide memo, assumed blame for the lapse. Zimmerman wasn't having any of it.

"You're jumping on the grenade to save your friend," he said.

"Setting a budget deadline for the new advertising was my call to make, not Irwin's," Steve replied. "It's as simple as that."

"You're covering for him," Andreas maintained.

"How was he supposed to pay for the new commercials?" Steve answered. "Monopoly money? Irwin couldn't get started until he had a budget to work with."

The franchise owners were equally skeptical. Many of them had met Irwin, and they were, almost to a person, put off by him. He lacked Steve's down-at-heel, empathetic nature. When it was rumored how much Irwin was making, that was all the information any of them needed to know.

Steve's maneuver ultimately worked. The assault of criticism was stemmed—at least for a time. Once again, Irwin was left to do what he did best, and now he was doing it with an expanded budget. But as a new year got under-way, Steve began to see elements of old problems beginning to reemerge. And what he saw was deeply troubling.

30

Relapse

With the onslaught of criticism, Irwin began slipping back into his old habits, growing increasingly dictatorial toward his staff. Two of his most talented people unexpectedly quit without giving a reason. When Steve looked into the matter, the creative director said that they could no longer work for Irwin.

"They found him impossible," he said. "When he gets frustrated he becomes a monster."

"Irwin?" Steve couldn't quite fathom this.

"The guy is bad news," the CD said. "When they resigned, Irwin shouted, *'Your ideas suck anyway!'* Wouldn't have believed it if I hadn't heard it with my own ears."

Steve didn't accept what he was being told at face value. More likely than not the creative director had his own agenda and found it convenient to exaggerate Irwin's idiosyncrasies to the boss.

But that was about to change.

A few days later, Steve dropped by Irwin's office. The department, it seemed, was in a strange state of disarray. Down the hall he overheard someone shouting, "We've got to come up with a new slogan!" Seconds later, the same voice was shouting, "This television time is off the charts … Haven't we already discussed buying more radio! *Why are we buying all of this television time when radio is the obvious bargain?"*

The person doing the shouting was Irwin, and the person being shouted at was none other than Margaret. Stunned, Steve ducked out of the office, unseen and unheard. Suddenly he found himself overcome with dread. His mind reeled as he rode the elevator down. He realized that he had an enormous problem on his hands, and he needed time to gather some facts and come up with an appropriate response.

Over the course of the next few days complaints began to circulate throughout the company, a few of which actually made it to Andreas's desk. Instead of approaching Irwin directly, Zimmerman took Steve to task, simply saying, "You've got a problem with your chief marketing officer."

"I know," Steve replied.

"Well then, fix it!" Andreas yelled.

Steve first went to Margaret to get her take on what was going on. By now he trusted both her judgment and her analysis, and he knew her relationship with Irwin to be grounded to reality and based on hard-earned respect. In spite of the abuse she had taken from him, Margaret would tell it like it was. So Steve brought her into his office, closed the door, and said, "We need to talk about our friend Irwin."

Margaret looked away and slowly nodded.

"All of the sniping about falling numbers has been getting to him," she said in a quiet, even voice. "He has a habit of becoming defensive when he's being criticized."

"So it's the criticism?"

"He also strikes people as …"—Margaret looked around the office, as though she might find the right description somewhere in the air—"… arrogant, I suppose is the word I'm after."

"Ah," Steve said. "Arrogant."

"It's a tough problem."

"We've dealt with a lot of tough problems."

"But this one is especially tough," Margaret said.

"Why is that?"

"Because Irwin really is superior," Margaret said with a hapless smile. "He's brilliant. Everyone knows it, and nobody is more aware of it than Irwin."

Steve was well aware of Irwin's value to the company. From the beginning he saw Irwin as being indispensable to the entire operation—and therefore to his own success. The last thing Steve wanted to do was to disturb the goose that had laid the golden egg. He just wanted that goose to keep producing more eggs. The best way to ensure this, Steve fatefully concluded, was to do nothing at all.

◆　　　◆　　　◆

As brilliant as Irwin's next campaign was, it became all too clear that marketing and advertising were still under-funded. What was needed, Steve realized, was for Zimmerman to nearly double the budget. The more money he put into advertising, the more revenues were driven. Steve also realized that, in spite of the recent success, Zimmerman still saw the advertising budget as an expense, one that he loudly exaggerated as being "my burden alone to bear." Getting him to double that burden was either unlikely or impossible. Nevertheless, Steve made his case to the boss. To his utter shock, however, Zimmerman saw Steve's point and signed off on the expanded budget without a word of protest.

But this was hardly the end of his troubles. When Steve arranged for a conference call with the franchisees, they had their own set of complaints with advertising.

"We loved the last run," an owner in Lake Forrest, Illinois said, "but it was expensive. The menu changes alone cost me $5,000."

An Italian-American owner in Fort Lauderdale had a less positive response, saying, "Why fix something that ain't broke?"

By now Steve had well established relationships with most of the franchisees, and it was a relationship grounded in success. As a result, they gave Steve the time of day to explain where the money would go; they seemed to appreciate it that corporate would be chipping. His pitch illustrated what these changes could do *for them*. A full third agreed on the spot to move forward, while another third sat on the fence, not entirely willing to take the chance, many of them skeptical of the campaign helping their operation to a meaningful degree; perhaps the money should go toward other things. The rest were adamant against adopting one expensive change after another, claiming they would be out of business "if the scheme didn't work."

"What if you had a say in the direction we were taking the company?" Steve asked.

The conference line was silent for a moment.

"What did you have in mind?" the Fort Lauderdale owner asked.

"The owners could form a committee," Steve said. "You would collaborate with the marketing department and have a hand in shaping the campaign."

There was more silence on the line, and then some murmuring among the owners. Steve knew that he now had their attention.

"We like that idea, Steve," someone said. "We like it a lot."

"We want to be continually improving the brand," Steve added.

After some murmuring, the Fort Lauderdale owners said, "We understand."

"Let's contact the other owners with the proposal," Steve said, "and then we'll talk about how to move forward."

31

A New Course

Later that afternoon Steve met with Irwin to tell him the good news.

"You offered them what?" was his old friend's response.

"I offered them a committee to develop ideas and suggestions on marketing and advertising," Steve said.

"Tell me you're joking."

"What's the problem?" Steve said, completely taken aback.

"So I'll be … *collaborating* with franchise owners? People who run restaurants for a living?"

Steve shrugged. "That's right."

Irwin let his head fall against his desktop. It made a *thud* upon contact.

"What's wrong with listening to them," Steve said. "They know the customers better than we do."

"But they don't know marketing from a hole in the ground," Irwin groaned as he slowly lifting his head. "And they think they do, which only compounds the problem."

"They're the people who generate every penny this company makes," Steve replied. "We have to keep that in mind."

"What does that have to do with anything?"

"Look. I had to give them something."

"So you handed them a monkey wrench …"

Steve couldn't quite get over what he was hearing. He'd been so sure that Irwin would be thrilled that Zimmerman and the owners were going to go along with the larger plan. So what if Irwin had to sit in on a couple of conference calls with a half-dozen owners?

"It's not too late to call it off," Steve said. "But they aren't going to cooperate without a seat at the table."

Irwin held his head in his hands.

"So it's an either-or scenario?" he mumbled.

"No one gets everything they want."
Irwin sat in silence, gloomily contemplating his choices.
"I'll take the larger budget," he whined.

◆   ◆   ◆

At the top of the week the owners approved a round of sweeping improvements, and three days later they elected a committee of seven of their peers to join Steve, Irwin and Irwin's team in Omaha for their first meeting. Evenly scattered across the country, they converged on the Midwest for two long days of brainstorming to develop the most effective and creative approach to selling the Antonio's restaurant experience to North Americans. It was here, around a conference table at a local Ramada near the airport, that Steve caught another glimpse of what Irwin's detractors had been quietly complaining about.

Steve and Irwin had flown out together on a direct flight from Kennedy to Omaha. From the beginning, Steve noticed that Irwin was strangely absent from his company. His attention was devoted to watching the weather moving over the Midwest, and the tablet on which he occasionally jotted a note. Whenever Steve asked him a question, Irwin offered fragmented answers. Little changed when they arrived at the Ramada. If anything, Irwin only became more detached. When the meeting convened the following morning at 9:00 a.m., Irwin was still in his room. He arrived after everyone had seated themselves around the conference table, sipping coffee and eating hotel pastries. Steve introduced Irwin as he ambled in looking forlorn, almost homesick.

"This is the creative mind," Steve said as Irwin took his seat, "behind the brilliant campaign that boosted company-wide revenues 11% last quarter."

The announcement was met with a smattering of applause, which Irwin acknowledged with a disconsolate grimace. The expression made it clear to everyone present that this was the last place on the planet that Irwin wanted to be. Steve noticed the franchise owner from Seattle rolling his eyes at Irwin. Several Midwestern owners exchanged knowing looks; they had Irwin pegged as the self-absorbed Madison Avenue type who took credit for making pretty commercials on a champagne budget. The meeting was all downhill from there.

What amazed Steve most about this meeting was how privy the owners were to Irwin's attitude and the emotions behind his arrogance. They knew that Irwin saw them as meddling in his field of expertise, territory he had staked out as his alone. And they were not afraid to let him know that they were of the unanimous opinion that they could do a better job.

So the stage was set for fireworks. The meeting got underway with a general discussion of what had worked in recent months and what had not.

"I think we can all agree that we're on a clear path to success," Steve said as he walked before the table. "And I think this is why the owners agreed to a sweeping new round of menu changes and restaurant improvements."

"I don't know about that," the Dallas franchise owner interrupted. "That's not why *I* agreed to it, and I don't think that's why anyone else did either."

Steve paused before the table.

"If your decision wasn't based on past success," he asked, "then why did you vote to authorize it?"

"I want to have a say in how we advertise in the future," he replied, as though surprised that Steve didn't realize this.

At this point Irwin caught Steve's eye, as if to say "I told you so."

"No more unfunded remodeling mandates!" an Atlanta owner chimed in.

"I really did not like that last campaign," the Chicago owner added.

"That campaign," Steve replied, "was exceedingly well received by the public."

"It was fine," the Dallas owner said. "But those remodeling changes cost each and every franchisee one hell of a lot of money."

Irwin aggressively straightened himself in his chair, unable to abide what he was hearing.

"The question each of you should be asking yourselves," he said in a very sharp tone, "is 'How much money did it make me?'"

"It made us some money," the Dallas owner conceded. "But the ROI wasn't what we thought it would be."

"I think we can do a whole lot better," the Seattle owner agreed.

Steve turned to Irwin who gave him a helpless shrug.

"I guess I'm not needed," Irwin said to the group.

"Don't be so defensive," snapped the Dallas owner with a sharp twang. "You've got some good ideas, but some of 'em are real dogs."

"Some are real *expensive* dogs," the Atlanta owner added.

"Most of those remodeling changes haven't made me a dime," the Los Angeles owner broke in, "and they cost me a pretty penny."

"I'd second that!" the Des Moines owner added. "And that's something I don't think you folks at the corporate office understand."

"Sometimes I can't quite believe what I'm being told I have to pay for!" the Cincinnati owner nearly shouted.

And so it went on and on … It would have kept going on indefinitely had Irwin not stood up and said, "I don't need to hear any more baseless complaints from a bunch of spaghetti cooks."

With that, Irwin left the room.

Steve didn't know whether to go talk to his old friend or stay in the conference room and put his owners in their place. For a moment he stood paralyzed with indecision before the franchisees.

"That Irwin fellow," the Dallas owner mumbled in his twang, "is so damned full of himself."

"That's not true," Steve said, startling the owner. "He's brilliant, and no one here seems to recognize what he's done for us."

"I wouldn't call him brilliant," the Los Angeles owner said. "He just picked some low hanging fruit with that campaign. Anybody could have done that."

"That," Steve said, "is definitely not the case. It's also not fair."

Dallas looked like he was about to say something, but thought better of it. The rest of the owners seemed to be casting a suspicious eye on Steve, as though perhaps they had been wrong about him from the beginning. Whose side was he really on? Theirs, or the side of the schmuck who had just insulted them and then stormed out of the room?

32

Golden Eggs

During the afternoon session, Irwin unexpectedly announced that he had to sit in on an extended conference call with advertising partners, and would miss the meeting. Steve was secretly relieved. In his friend's absence at the meeting he decided to take an opportunity, and asked the owners to pay special attention to what he was about to say. Then, trying not to mince his words, he tried to tell them what he thought of their behavior toward their "gifted marketing executive."

"Stand down," he said as politely as he could. "Take it easy on Irwin for your own benefit, and for the benefit of the company."

"He thinks he has all the answers," the Atlanta owner said, "so we were just giving him the feedback that you failed to deliver."

"This isn't the way forward," Steve replied, quietly fuming. "This company was falling apart before Irwin came aboard, and now it's succeeding. This isn't an accident, and none of you should take that success for granted."

The owners seemed to accept the message, albeit reluctantly. The meeting ended with less controversial business, and there was the general feeling that at least some good work had gotten done. Before the meeting concluded, however, Steve again reminded everyone of Irwin's value to the company, saying, "Let's not kill the goose that laid the golden egg."

Apparently the admonition hit its mark. The following morning, several owners actually approached Irwin in the hotel lobby before heading to the airport, and apologized for what had been said. A few of them actually appeared to mean it. Irwin grinned, nodded, and accepted the gesture. But it meant little enough to him. He wasn't about to forgive or forget.

◆   ◆   ◆

Irwin brought home with him a slow burning anger. From his first hour back on the job, he became increasingly belligerent toward his senior staff, even toward his closest allies, such as Margaret. Steve noticed that the team's work instantly began to suffer. Deadlines were missed, and the departments seemed to be in a heightened state of disarray. Irwin attacked every member of his team as well as the franchise owners. On a few occasions he even attacked Steve. For his part, Steve noticed that Irwin never took accountability for the current state of business, and acted as though everyone in the organization was wrong—except himself. It was as though the abusive feedback Irwin had received from the owners in Omaha had shaken his confidence. As his anger simmered, his brilliance slowly began to desert him. He was no longer dreaming up campaigns; he was plotting revenge.

This correlation between conflict and underperformance was gradually but increasingly supported by revenues. Within a month of their return, Steve noticed that the numbers were beginning to trail off. And the problem only got worse as one quarter after another passed by. Zimmerman, who could not have cared less about Irwin's feelings, grew increasingly alarmed as each succeeding campaign marketing and culinary initiative bombed. His response to Steve on the matter was quintessential Andreas: "You need to get rid of him."

Deep down Steve knew that Zimmerman had a point, and the thought disturbed him. As a result, Steve couldn't bring himself to admit it or even deal with it. He knew he lacked the kind of creativity that Irwin had in abundance. Not only was this creativity something Steve didn't have, but it was something that he and the company now needed in order to survive.

Thus Zimmerman's command filled Steve with stark terror, because he didn't know how, in Andreas's words, to "get rid of him" without losing the key element to the company's success. So he was faced with what looked like an insolvable dilemma. Not only was Irwin the problem, he was also the solution. Without Irwin, Steve believed the business would fail within six months.

Even with Irwin on board, things had begun to go horribly wrong. The energy that had fueled the company's previous success was now dispersed in a thousand unproductive directions. Irwin sarcastically complained on a daily basis about the relentless telephone calls from owners across the country who were "sharing their brilliant ideas with me." In many cases they were not "sharing" so much as telling

Irwin what to do. Some of them acted as though Irwin was their personal assistant.

"Yesterday the Cedar Rapids owner was demanding that I put his daughter in my commercial!" Irwin nearly shouted. "He said I owed it to him because of all the money *he* pays *me!*"

"Oh God," Steve said, rubbing his temples.

"Can you believe it? He thinks that *he* is paying *me!*"

Steve could see the bad blood spreading, and it made him heartsick. Upon making the demand, the Cedar Rapids owner instantly incurred the full force of Irwin's wrath. After slamming down the telephone, the owner then shared the story with a few of his fellow owners—but neglected to mention his demand that Irwin hire his daughter for an Antonio's commercial. This dialogue reinforced the franchisees' beliefs that Irwin was an arrogant, overpaid jackass.

Steve couldn't get over how quickly the situation began to deteriorate. It threatened to spin entirely out of control when Steve began receiving complaints by telephone from owners everywhere demanding that something had to be done about Irwin. Steve's leadership abilities were now being put to the test, as he explained the situation to anyone who would listen, giving a fuller account of Irwin's value and potential to the company, and explaining the misunderstanding among the franchise owners. When they responded with the demand that Steve fire Irwin, Steve countered with pure pragmatism.

"He puts money in the cash register," he said. "He produces results."

"Not lately," the Atlanta owner countered.

And he had a point, one that was supported by the balance sheets. But Irwin was the expert, Steve told himself, and he was going to stand by his friend's side until the last dog had died.

33

Always Swing for the Fences

Steve knew that this problem wasn't going to just go away. In fact, it would only grow as the drumbeat of criticism leveled against Irwin intensified and his performance deteriorated. The company, Steve understood, was caught in a self-perpetuating cycle of criticism that crushed performance, which in turn only generated more criticism. Matters were soon brought to a head when Zimmerman called Steve into his office and weighed in on the Irwin matter in the form of a directive to Steve.

"Go find a new CMO," Andreas said in a shockingly direct closed-door meeting, "and throw Irwin out."

And that was that. Andreas then reached for his telephone to discuss another matter with another one of his business interests on another continent. As far as Andreas was concerned, the meeting was over.

Steve went directly from Andreas's office to Irwin's, rehearsing on the taxi ride over how he was going to broach the subject of his termination. This, he realized, was going to be the most difficult conversation of his professional life.

As the cab swept him uptown, Steve went over what he was going to say. Irwin could still be effective, he reminded himself. As much as I don't like his style, we're still getting results. He's the smartest, most creative person I know. Yes, he can be abusive. Yes, he can be aggressive. But he knows how to put money in the register. It isn't as much money as it once was, *but at least he knows how to make the cash registers ring …* This was the most salient fact, and it was being obscured by something as petty as a clash of personalities. And this is what gave this crisis its sadly ironic dimension: not only did Irwin know how to make the company successful, he was the only person in the company who possessed the magic.

With these thoughts foremost in Steve's mind, he approached Irwin's office with an overwhelming sense of apprehension. As he rose up in the elevator to Irwin's floor, he reminded himself that he didn't want to alienate the one person he depended upon most to drive the company toward success.

When Steve arrived at the office, Irwin happened to be putting the finishing touches on a new series of television and radio commercials he'd been working on for the past three months. It was a colossal project. When Steve poked his head into the office, Irwin excitedly waved him in. Steve found Margaret sitting before the blank screen of a television set, her gaze cast down to a notepad resting on her knee, her eyes never meeting Steve's. She was clearly distraught. She didn't have to say as much, but the source of her unhappiness was someone for whom they both cared deeply.

"You couldn't have picked a better moment to stop by," Irwin said as he slapped Steve on the back. "I just received the television tapes, and Margaret and I were just about to go over them together."

Caught off guard, Steve took the seat Irwin offered. Before he knew it, the television was playing the new commercials. There were three in all, and Steve could not help but be staggered by their cleverness and quality. Once again, this was vintage Irwin, Steve told himself. He demonstrates his brilliance when you least expected it. Zimmerman and every franchise owner was going to love these commercials.

"So what do you think?" Steve asked Margaret.

Without looking him in the eyes, Margaret said very somberly, "They're remarkable. In fact, I would say they're the best restaurant commercials I've ever seen."

Steve responded to Margaret's answer, simply saying, "Agreed."

But then Margaret was silent.

Steve and Irwin exchanged a puzzled look.

"Are you all right?" Irwin asked her.

"Quite all right," he said. Then she rose and added, "I've got a thousand things to deal with this morning ..."

Once she was gone, Irwin stepped behind his desk, put his hands on his hips. "So you really like them?" he asked, referring to the commercials.

Steve paused before answering.

"I love them," he said. "In fact, I think it's the best work you've ever done."

Irwin threw his hands in the air.

"I was swinging for the fences," he said.

"You always are," Steve replied.

Then Irwin noticed that Steve was staring at the door which Margaret had left ajar.

"Everything all right?" Irwin asked.

As Steve sat there, he realized that it might be best to say nothing for the moment. The commercials were in the can. Once everyone saw them, perhaps they would understand what he had understood all along—that Irwin was indispensable to this company.

"What's the matter?" Irwin asked again.

Steve shook his head.

"Nothing at all," he replied. "So when do you think we can send copies to Andreas and the owners?"

"Today," Irwin said, as though puzzled by the question.

"That's great," Steve said. "You're going to make a lot of people really happy."

34

A New World

Steve's final comment to his friend wasn't exactly on the mark, and he knew it. While everyone was dazzled by the brilliance of the commercials, they failed to properly attribute their genius to Irwin.

"Big productions like these are collaborative efforts by nature," Andreas noted to Steve. "A lot of people put a lot of time into them."

So Irwin was rewarded with a reprieve rather than a pardon. The reprieve was even extended when the commercials hit the airwaves and the registers started ringing. But Steve knew that the blizzard of receipts was not going to last forever, and once it had run its course, Irwin would again be fighting for his job.

Steve was right. In fact, the blizzard ended sooner than anyone had anticipated, and what followed was difficult for Steve to witness. As business fell off, company headquarters was once again beset with internal strife. The atmosphere wasn't any better, Steve observed, than when he had first arrived. Perhaps it was even a little worse. Everyone was angry with everyone else, and all of the discontent seemed to flow from the same source—Irwin's cluttered head. And yet Steve could not bring himself to initiate a search for a new CMO. When Zimmerman learned that Irwin was still with the company, he immediately connected it to the falling numbers. That's when he called Steve to a meeting at his office.

The abrupt nature of the call puzzled Steve. He supposed that it was about the tumbling numbers, and assumed he would have to come up with some sort of explanation for his boss.

"So tell me," Andreas said. "What's your biggest problem? Why is Irwin still around?"

"We have several problems," Steve began, "one of which is increased—"

"Increased competition is not the problem and you know it."

If Steve had had any doubts as to why Andreas had called this meeting, they were now gone.

"I know what you're getting at," Steve replied.

"Your problem isn't with marketing and advertising. Your problem is with Irwin."

"It's more complicated than that."

"It's not more complicated," Andreas snapped. And then he bore down hard on his CEO. "Indeed, it's all quite simple. I've been letting you run the company as you see fit, but now you're not doing what you need to do. Irwin has got to go."

"I told you before, I can't just let him … *go* …"

"Yes you can," Zimmerman said. "It happens all the time. Companies fire people who do not perform. Irwin was good for a while, but he's not anymore. The owners don't like him for their own reasons, and I don't like him because he's costing me money. No one at corporate likes him either."

"Forget about the franchise owners for a minute," Steve replied. "This is about bottom-line performance."

Andreas was no longer listening to what he had to say, which gave Steve the sense that he had nothing to lose.

"I'm not getting rid of Irwin," he said flatly.

Andreas folded his hands in his lap and sat bolt-upright. Steve could hear him breathing from where he sat across the desk.

"You won't fire your friend."

"I won't fire *Irwin* because he's good for this company."

"He's bringing *us* down," Andreas said. "He's bringing *me* down."

"He's still good, and I need him. Especially now that we have twenty-one direct competitors. Two years ago we had four."

Andreas's fierce gaze slowly softened. Against all expectations, he appeared to be taking a moment to give serious consideration to what his CEO was telling him.

"I don't like him," Andreas said under his breath. "He either changes or he's out."

"I'll talk to Irwin."

"I don't want you to *talk* to him," Andreas said with grave seriousness. "I want you to fire him."

"Just let me see what I can do to get through to him."

Andreas responded with silence. He sensed that his CEO was going to try to finesse another reprieve for his friend. And he was absolutely correct. Steve interpreted the equivocal silence as permission to keep Irwin on. And with that, Steve took the opportunity to slip quietly out of his boss's office before anything more was said.

35

The Ambivalent Boss

That afternoon Steve called Irwin and invited him out to lunch at a small Thai restaurant in Soho. There, surrounded by the eerily serene waitstaff, the scent of curry, and corpulent brass Buddhas, he told Irwin of his conversation with Andreas.

"He wants you gone," Steve said. "So do the franchisees and a significant number of the corporate staff."

"Well …"

There was a long silence. The waitress came and took their orders, bowed, and disappeared, leaving Steve and Irwin sitting across from one another with this strange emotional fog between them.

"I've actually got something that could pull us out of the doldrums," Irwin finally said.

Steve abruptly looked up from his menu.

"It's not about ideas anymore."

"It's never too late for a great idea," Irwin said casually.

"It would have to be something that will boost sales immediately," Steve said, thoroughly exasperated.

Irwin nodded confidently.

"What is it?" Steve asked.

"A combination of LTOs [Limited Time Offers], bounce-back coupons, and dual branding," Irwin said.

"Sounds good," Steve said, "Keep going."

"The LTOs and coupons will spark business right away, while the dual branding will keep the marketing costs to a minimum."

"Who would be our branding partners?" Steve asked.

"I've been in contact with a soft drink company and an up-market pasta outfit. They're all people I've worked with in the past."

"Okay …"

"Zimmerman will see a quick spike in business with the LTOs and coupons, and he and the owners won't be hit with any additional costs for marketing initiatives because they'll be shared."

"You could try."

"So everybody will be happy."

Steve found himself grinning. He hadn't, in Zimmerman's words, "taken Irwin out." And once again Irwin was going to try to pull a rabbit out of his hat in the eleventh hour.

But deep down Steve knew it was too late. Over the course of lunch, he let his friend know it.

◆   ◆   ◆

For the first time in his career, Steve's job felt exceedingly … *provisional*. After years of being thought of as a superstar, he was now just hanging on, trying to get through one more quarter. And the fact that he was just trying to keep his job caused him a great deal of anguish. Irwin could succeed this time around, and even succeed in a big way, and yet it would buy him only a few months. If Irwin's next project failed, it was sure to be all over. There would be no debate with Zimmerman about what could be done. There wouldn't be so much as a heated discussion.

This realization brought a new level of stress to Steve's life. He and Irwin were going to make the franchise owners a lot of money, and they were still probably going to lose their jobs. This is what it came down to. Perhaps Steve had always been operating under the perform-or-die rule, and was only realizing it now that the quality of his performance was being called into question. In business, you either succeed or you simply go away. It was all very clear to him now.

In any event, Steve now began suffering anxiety attacks that beset him in the middle of the night. He was racked with insomnia as he padded about his home, imagining the scene of his family moving into a house in Brooklyn, and suggesting to Susan that she might have go back to work. And that made his blood run cold.

It also elicited a painful stomach ulcer. He would rise up out of bed while Susan slept, take a bottle of antacid, and guzzle it down. He didn't want to share his anxiety with her for fear of keeping her up at night as well. So she slept while he aimlessly wandered about, haunting the catacombs of his house night after night. But as he walked about the half-lit rooms, he came to a few important realizations.

He finally understood just how psychologically dependent upon Irwin he had become. Steve's value to the company no longer depended upon his own performance. It depended on Irwin's. For the first time in his career, Steve's destiny was no longer in his own hands. No matter what he did, no matter how well he performed in his various duties as CEO, his survival was inextricably linked to the overall success of Irwin's marketing ideas, and this was the realization that struck so directly at Steve's sense of self-worth. He felt helpless, and this, as much as any of his other worries, was what kept him up at night. He no longer felt like the wunderkind who had made one brilliant call after another as an analyst, or the manager who had saved an entire manufacturing plant that provided jobs for some 300 men and women. He was now the anxious, frightened and cowering CEO who prayed every night that he wouldn't be fired in the morning.

36

Transition

In the coming weeks it became increasingly clear to Andreas Zimmerman that his company's grand effort toward building a national brand had come to very little. All of the expense and trouble he had assumed in the last few years had bought him a diminishing piece of market share in the restaurant business. He had owned the company for about half the time he had originally planned, and now, according to his accountants, it was only worth somewhere between 7% and 10% more than what he had paid for it. But even this was open to question. He'd made enormous investments in marketing and advertising, and had received a hodgepodge of successful and failed campaigns that had developed little in the way of brand cohesion and sales momentum. As disappointing as the revelation was for Andreas, it also clarified his financial picture and simplified his decision-making process.

While Andreas plotted his next move, Steve took his family to New Hampshire and stayed at an inn on Lake Winnipesaukee. He thought that getting out of the city would perhaps let him at least sleep a few hours.

It didn't.

During his time at the lake, Steve felt his depression closing in around him. While Susan and Sarah slept, he padded about the creaky old Victorian inn, and in the morning, he took out a small wooden sailboat and lazily cruised with his family around the lake in a faint breeze. Susan noticed that he wasn't very "present" and asked him what the matter was. His answer was always the same, always "some nonsense at work."

Not wanting to push too hard, Susan left it at that. Steve could sense his wife backing away, allowing him some psychological space to ponder what she could only assume were difficult matters, and he loved her for it.

But Steve wasn't merely thinking things through. This was a deepening depression he was dealing with, and it was always there, always looming in the background in the form of a relentless feeling of dread. And some sixth sense told him that things were going to get crazy when he returned to New York City.

On their last evening at the lake Steve sauntered down to the end of the dock and stared at the water. Here he watched a boy fishing with a bamboo pole. His eye was drawn to the red-and-white bobber floating on the surface. Suddenly a fish struck, and the bobber was pulled under. Steve thought to himself, *This is me. Helplessly waiting to be pulled under the surface at any moment by a large, lurking fish.* Later that evening Susan found her husband there at the end of the dock.

"Is everything all right?" she asked, as she came up behind him.

He didn't answer, and this alarmed her.

"Steve?" she said again, putting a hand on his shoulder.

He turned to her.

"What's wrong?"

Steve just sat there, his feet dangling over the side of the mossy wooden planks, gazing vacantly at the water's reflective surface.

"Work has been a little difficult lately," was all he would offer.

Susan turned to face him squarely, and then leveled her gaze.

"Tell me what's going on."

Steve hesitated. Then he realized that Susan deserved to know what was happening, and so he told her, studiously neglecting to convey the seriousness of the problem. But at least she would know what the problem was. When he mentioned Irwin's name, he could see how the news surprised her. Nevertheless, once he'd finished, she was smiling, and what she had to say shocked him.

"You have to do what's right for the company," she said in a soft voice. "That's your job."

Steve nodded. He knew Susan was right.

37

Decision

To Steve's surprise, things seemed to have quieted down over the weekend, and Irwin's behavior once again retreated into the background. By the end of the week he decided to postpone his talk with Irwin for a few days. A week later he quietly decided to postpone it indefinitely.

But there had been two significant developments, neither of which Steve was privy to. The first involved Zimmerman. Andreas had been keeping an eye on Steve and had noticed with mounting exasperation his paralysis in finding qualified candidates to replace Irwin. Irwin, Zimmerman silently concluded, was only a symptom of his company's problem. The root cause was his CEO.

The other development involved Margaret. In an uncharacteristically secretive move, she called an old acquaintance of hers who was now an executive consultant. In a very long and detailed conversation, she conveyed to him the nature of Steve's troubles with Irwin, the company, and with Steve's state of mind.

"The problem could very well bring down the company," she confided at the end of the discussion. "Something has to be done right away."

The consultant she had called was Yours Truly, Edward A. Meagher III.

◆   ◆   ◆

Margaret had seen the problem from its inception. She had seen the full potential of its threat, and she had seen the threat develop. Now it was being realized.

She also knew that I was an acquaintance and admirer of Steve's from the dawn of his career. Margaret and I both knew how talented he was. We both knew of his unusual (and in my opinion, brilliant) approach to business (in fact, many of his business values would eventually find their way into my business model). As an executive consultant and coach, Margaret understood that I would not have any interests that conflicted with solving the problem.

"I want you to talk to Steve," she said.

120

Then she laid out the situation, offering her analysis in considerable detail. We talked for nearly two hours, and the entire time I was struck by her loyalty to Steve. She clearly had his best interests in mind, and those interests were congruous with those of the company. The conversation finally ended with her saying, "He needs to save himself for the sake of the organization."

"I'll be here," was all I could say to that.

I didn't have to wait long.

Steve called later that night. We briefly caught up on one another's lives, after which there was an extended silence. Steve, I sensed, was in a state of anguish.

"Margaret called me earlier this afternoon," I finally said.

"I don't know what to do," he murmured.

"Yes you do," I replied.

Steve was again silent.

"And what is that?" he asked. There was a note of skepticism in his voice. His problem, he was convinced, had no solution.

"You need to demonstrate that you're looking out for your employees, your investors—and for yourself."

"Look," Steve said. "I don't know what Margaret told you, but this guy has saved my bacon year after year. It would kill him *and* me to let him go."

"I have a question for you," I said.

"Go ahead."

"What good is it going to do anyone if you lose your job?"

Steve wouldn't answer. I'd obviously touched a nerve, and with that, the conversation quickly petered out.

Two days passed without another call from Margaret or Steve. Then, out of the blue, Steve was on the line. Without any preamble whatsoever, he said, "Zimmerman is threatening to fire me. He says I have to make up my mind. I have to either support him or support Irwin."

"So what are you going to do?" I asked.

"*What do you mean by that?*" Steve erupted. *What makes him think he can do this to me? I'm not that far from the end of my contract, and a potential $2 million payout. And now he's threatening me with this?*"

"He's been threatening you with it for a while though, hasn't he?"

The line was dead silent.

"What will Susan say?" I finally asked.

"What do you mean?"

"What will Susan say when you go home and tell her that Zimmerman fired you today because you didn't listen to him? You didn't listen to your colleagues, and you didn't listen to the company's shareholders. Worst of all, you didn't even listen to your own gut. Steve, what will Susan say when you tell her you put Irwin above everyone—above even her and your daughter?"

In a very soft voice, Steve whispered, "Where do you come off saying that?"

I thought about what I was doing for a moment. Instead of changing course, however, I decided to step it up. I needed to demonstrate loyalty to Steve—even if it meant jeopardizing our friendship. What Steve needed was a strong dose of reality.

"The only person you're putting first is Irwin. The only interests you have in mind are his. You don't have the company's interests in mind, you don't have Zimmerman's. What I find incredible is that you don't even have your *own* in mind. That's totally inexplicable to me. That tells me something is deeply wrong with your thinking."

Steve was now seething. I could hear him on the other end of the line—almost wheezing—barely able to contain his rage.

"Certainly it's in Susan's best interest if you keep your job, isn't it?"

"You know," Steve said. "I thought you could help, Ed. But calling you has been a mistake."

"So what are you going to tell Susan?" I asked. "You can hang up after you tell me, but that's what I really want to know."

"Screw you," he yelled.

A second later the line went dead.

I sat behind my desk for a long moment, and re-ran the conversation over in my mind. After going over what I had said and how I had said it, I concluded that it had been the right approach. It was absolutely necessary that I get through to Steve, as he simply wasn't thinking rationally about his predicament. He was feeling so helpless and confused that he had lost his grasp on the nature of his problem. Clearly he was defensive and had lashed out—but this too was a symptom of his despair. What he needed was a kick in the pants, and that was what I had given him. What I had offered was an expression of pure loyalty to him, and without it he simply wasn't going to listen to what he needed to hear. Nevertheless, I have to admit that my stomach was churning and my hands were beginning to sweat as I pondered the situation. I wanted to pick up the telephone to explain myself, and perhaps even apologize, but I knew that if I didn't put some time and space around this challenge, the message might not sink in to Steve's head. So I stared at the phone and resisted the temptation to pick it up.

At ten o'clock the following morning, Steve called me back.

"I just wanted you to know that I fired my good friend this morning," he said in an excruciatingly sorrowful voice. "It was the hardest thing I've ever done in my life."

"What changed your mind?"

"Last night Susan and Sarah were asleep in our bed when I came home," he said. "I just stood there watching them, thinking of what you said, and that's when it hit me that you were right. I had to fire my friend. There was no other course of action I could take."

"How are you feeling now?" I asked.

"You know," he said with a faintly philosophical note, "not as bad as I thought I would."

His voice was strangely calm, serene. Somehow it seemed "off," and as we talked I was slowly overcome by a sense of foreboding. Something was wrong. Somehow I sensed that this was the calm before a very fearsome storm.

38

Loyalists Do Not Let Each Other Fail

I wish this story had a happy ending, but in real life not all endings are.

A few days later I received another call. It was Steve. He was calling from his home, because a few hours earlier he too had been fired. His voice was cracking. I asked him what happened, and the story he related was heartbreaking.

◆   ◆   ◆

Zimmerman had called Steve to his office and immediately threw down a spreadsheet with the year's numbers. While Steve was looking them over, Zimmerman went on a tear: "How many times did I tell you to get rid of Irwin?"

Steve just stood there, frozen. Zimmerman screamed at him for twenty minutes about how the franchisees were furious. Shareholders were calling him around the clock, and the bottom line was no better than it had been three years ago when he'd gotten into this whole mess.

"You were supposed to be my golden boy!" Andreas shouted. "I had huge plans for you that went way beyond Antonio's ... and now you're nothing to me—except gone!"

◆   ◆   ◆

Now, on the other end of the line, Steve's voice fell silent.

"Steve," I finally said in a firm tone, "what happened to you? Back in the day you would've handled this whole situation so differently. What changed?"

Steve cleared his throat.

"I'm not sure," he said. "One mistake led to another, and eventually snowballed out of control. I'm so disappointed in myself ... When I fired Irwin, I gave him a big severance package. It turns out he's been interviewing for a while, and already has a new job lined up. Before he starts he's taking his family to Hawaii for a month-long vacation. Meanwhile, I'm on my way home to tell my wife that I botched up our future … The thought of breaking the news to Susan is far more painful than anything Zimmerman can throw at me."

"Not that this is any consolation," I said, "but *you are* brilliant. You're one of the greatest guy's I've ever known, and you've been a mentor and a friend to me for twenty years. Granted, today is a really bad day, but you *will* land on your feet. I have total confidence in you."

We talked for a while longer, and I tried to coach him on how to handle things with Susan. But I wasn't worried about them. They had a completely solid, loving relationship.

After we hung up, I sat back in my chair and folded my hands behind my head. While it saddened me to know that a good friend was going through such a difficult time, the moment was also an epiphany. As I sat there, I decided to take a look at my work in progress, the Woodstone High-Performance Model. This was something that I had been in the process of putting together for years, and it had yet to be truly complete. But this was the moment that I grasped something very important. When I incorporated my thoughts, I felt like it was finally coming together for the first time. At last I could summarize the heart and soul of the Woodstone Model, the idea at its very core: "Loyalists do not let each other fail."

◆   ◆   ◆

Loyalists do not let each other fail. This would become the central concept of the model.

Had I known that Steve was in this predicament sooner, I could have helped him. I also knew I was pushing his buttons by asking him "What will Susan say?" But this is what any loyalist would do. I knew that he would be mad at me for pushing him, but I felt I had an obligation to get him to do the right thing, and that obligation required that I ask him very relevant but very difficult questions. The most relevant of these questions, the one that struck at the heart of the matter, was: "What will Susan say?"

Oftentimes in a loyalist relationship, one person will say something that simply needs to be said; but it's also something that could potentially jeopardize the friendship. That is what loyal people do for each other. We are more comfortable doing this with our children, our spouses, even our best friends; the Woodstone

High Performance Model™ takes this principle a step further and teaches that we need to do this with our coworkers as well.

I spent twenty-four years in corporate America, and no matter what level I was at or which company I worked for, one thing always rang true: I was absolutely dependent on the people around me for my own success. It's an interesting dynamic when you think about it. We spend the majority of our lives—from high school to college and beyond—trying to achieve the personal success that will one day land us the Big Job. Once we get it, our first task is to put aside our personal accomplishments and agenda for the good of the team and the company. But this seldom occurs. Why? Because we've been taught that individual success has nothing to do with teamwork. For more than a quarter century, I looked on as one brilliant executive after another rose up through the ranks only to fail just as his or her ship came in.

Steve had been an inspiration to me throughout my career. He was good with people, and I was struck by what I considered to be his revolutionary management style. What I admired most was his ability to understand who he needed to be for each individual in his life. Let's face it. We are all different. We all have strengths and weaknesses. Because of this, we have to be "handled" in a certain way in order to perform at our highest level. Steve understood this intuitively at the very earliest stages of his career.

Another central component of the Woodstone coaching method is a personality analysis and team personality analysis, both of which use the Myers Briggs Type Indicator, or the MBTI. When I first decided to start Woodstone Consulting, I knew that I would incorporate the MBTI, as I had used it throughout the course of my career, and knew it was a powerful tool that explained personality preferences. I knew that it would be helpful to *demonstrate*—and not just *tell*—executives that they were innately different from one another.

You might wonder why this would be helpful to an executive. The answer is simple. During the MBTI "test" each person's differences are categorized into their various strengths and weaknesses. The reason that this tool is so effective is because it teaches people about others by teaching them something about themselves. We humans are creatures of habit, and we all have different needs. Thus, it's a valuable experience to get together with a group of people and explain to them their own behaviors and the behaviors of those around them. My clients are amazed by how precisely the MBTI describes their personality preferences, which helps illustrate just how different their peers and subordinates are from them. It also allows them to see the critical need to understand personality when it comes to team development. And this is how you drive business to a whole new level. A particular combination of personalities on a team can be harnessed to produce a cohesive unit that performs at a much higher level than it otherwise would.

Here's a very simple example. The MBTI identifies me as both an "extrovert" and as a "feeler." My wife has also taken the test, and she too is an extrovert and a feeler. Why is this important? It tells us we have certain traits in common. We are both extroverts, which means we both get our energy from others. We are both feelers, which means we make our decisions based on circumstances instead of facts. However, we differ in two dichotomies. According to the test, I am more "intuitive," whereas she is more "sensing." The intuitive person sees the big picture, while the sensing person is very detail-oriented. I tell my clients that the difference lies in the way two people interpret a mosaic. The intuitive person sees the mosaic as a whole, whereas the sensing person sees the individual tiles.

Once you understand that others naturally see the world differently, you come to understand why this is a good thing and a benefit to an organization (in this case, my marriage). It's useful to me to know that my wife needs to have access to more details in our daily life, while it's useful for her to understand that I only need to see the big picture. Knowing this about one another makes us more compatible, and therefore a better husband-and-wife team. The same, of course, is true for larger organizations, such as a multinational corporation.

However, there is a catch. One can never allow one's "profile" to become an excuse. A case in point would be Irwin. The marketing team went to him on several occasions, telling him that, while his ideas were brilliant, what they needed from him were priorities and a method for implementing them. But he refused to give them what they needed. Instead, he arrogantly claimed over and over that he was the "idea guy." In his mind, this was his profile, if you will, the extent of who he was, and it was all he thought he had to be. He would have been far more successful had he been able to see things from the perspective of the people around him and see what they needed from him. To his mind he was strictly a brainstorming machine, which resulted not only in his own demise, but that of the company.

Steve's thinking was the antithesis of Irwin's. When I think about his relationship with Ivan Kowalski, I marvel at his willingness to put himself in the hands of a blue-collar worker simply to gain knowledge and experience. At some level he understood that he and the Gunther Company would fail if he didn't go through this process with this one key employee. He realized that Ivan was intimidated by his youth and education, and that the only way to make someone like Ivan a loyalist was to work next to him and sweat with him. In time, Ivan would come to put all of his trust in Steve, and would have followed him to the gates of hell.

Simply put, that is the benchmark of the loyalty necessary to succeed in business. Think about it: without Ivan's unshakable support, Steve would have failed. His career would have ended right there on the manufacturing floor.

Another fundamental Woodstone concept has to do with the people we are surrounded by throughout our career. They are some of the people we know best, and they can be placed in three distinct categories. The first is the *loyalist*, the person who will do whatever it takes to help us succeed. These are the people we want to be surrounded by—and the more of them we have the better. The second category is what I call the *ambivalent*, the person who doesn't care enough to go out of his or her way for us. This person is neither a *loyalist*, nor are they out to see us fail. We simply don't matter to them. The third category of individual is the most caustic to our careers and peace of mind—the *saboteur*. These are the people who delight in watching us fail.

We've all had experiences with each person in these categories, and we know what they can each do *for* and *to* us. It is important to have as many loyalists in our lives as possible. Steve didn't have a name for these people in his life, but early on in his career he figured out that he needed them. Incredibly, he also knew how to turn saboteurs and the ambivalent into loyalists. He did this by figuring out what each individual person around him needed, and he followed up by giving it to them. In short, he empowered them with the ability to succeed, which ultimately accounted for his own success. And this is where the Woodstone Model comes full-circle: You become successful by making those around you successful, by being a loyalist and cultivating loyalist relationships. This is something Steve understood at the beginning of his career. The opposite, of course, is also true, and this was a lesson he learned when it ended.

Epilogue

The story unfolded over the years was telling. Irwin went on to a new company, but was soon inflicting the same psychological sabotage on nearly everyone with whom he came in contact. The new advertising shop, however, wasn't nearly as accommodating as Steve had been, which they demonstrated by dismissing Irwin before his first year was up. Desperate to find a job, he took yet another position as creative director at another agency at a greatly reduced salary, but was once again let go. This time he took it upon himself to start his own agency, which floundered for two years before failing altogether. This was a shame, as his concepts were as brilliant as ever. He simply couldn't find anyone who was both talented and willing to execute them on his behalf. Nor could he find clients who would endure a steady diet of abuse. The moment his relationships with those around him failed, so did he.

Steve, on the other hand, took the general manager post at the Boston-based Seville Ice Cream Company, and made a fraction of his former salary. With his departure, Zimmerman instituted a search campaign for Steve's replacement as well as Irwin's. Irwin's successor was a breath of fresh air at headquarters, especially for Margaret. But Steve's replacement was not. Indeed, he was roundly rejected by the franchisees, Margaret, and everyone but Andreas. Once again, Antonio's soon found itself in a state of perpetual turmoil. By now Zimmerman just wanted to be rid of the business altogether, and finally sold it to a Kuwaiti firm after having invested several millions into his company over the course of nearly six years. Through the entire painful process he failed to turn a meaningful profit.

After six years of headaches, Europe's new kid on the block was none the richer. Indeed, he was a good deal poorer. It wasn't in his personality to look reflectively upon why this was, or why things had worked out the way they had. Instead, he consigned the experience to memory as an unpleasant dream, one he simply hoped not to relive. But he inevitably would. Once his reputation for tyranny had been firmly established throughout New York and Europe, he found the number of talented people who were willing to work with him to be exceedingly small indeed. His problems were like a frustrating headwind—an invisible force that he could feel but not see, and that was always working against him.

His problems also had the compounding effect of magnifying his dictatorial nature, and soon he was losing money with each passing quarter in nearly every sector of his business empire. In short order, his wife left him, taking with her a good portion of what remained of his fortune. Six years after selling Antonio's, Andreas retreated back to Dusseldorf where he took a post as a venture capitalist, doing what he had once done with his own money. His name slipped from society pages without notice, as he was just another investment banker looking to turn a deal, just one of the many thousands.

Steve, of course, had missed his big payday. He was no longer as marketable as he had once been, but Susan was never going to leave him no matter how spectacularly he failed, and he knew it. This gave him a confidence and peace of mind that Zimmerman would never know. But Steve also understood that his professional and financial life had fallen far short of what could have been, and he would always be aware of this fact. Reflecting back on his tenure at Antonio's, he too came to realize that his failure had something to do with his misplaced loyalty. He failed shareholders, employees, his family, and ultimately himself.

Again, Steve's story is hardly unique. Indeed, it's part of a phenomenon that I've been a witness to throughout my entire business career. Each episode proved to be an excruciatingly painful ordeal for everyone involved, and I've always viewed it as so completely and utterly unnecessary. To me it's tragic simply because it is avoidable.

Perhaps the one person who did her best to hold this broken company together was Margaret. A few years after Steve left, however, she grew weary of the tiresome franchise owners, and the endless parade of new CEOs who did not value her wisdom and had no idea what it took for a company like this to succeed. At age fifty-six she took a post as an adjunct professor at the NYU business school and relaxed in a comfortable and rewarding academic lifestyle. She came to love her students, and they loved her. She didn't make much money, but she realized that she now had her life back. And after mending so many relationships at Antonio's for so many years, all of the relationships in her private life seemed so easy, manageable and rewarding. Companies come, and unfortunately companies go. And companies, of course, are made up of people, a precious resource that has to be managed with a great deal of care.

About the Authors

Edward A. Meagher III worked in labor relations for ITT Communications, and went on to become Vice President of Human Resources for KFC USA, a division of PepsiCo, Inc. He is also the founder of the Woodstone Consulting, an enormously successful executive consulting and coaching company. In 1999 Meagher became a consultant to the U.S. Nordic Combined Ski Team, which selected the Woodstone Leadership Model for the 2000 World Cup and the 2002 Winter Olympic Games in Salt Lake City. Today Meagher works with corporate teams at the Woodstone Ranch, and speaks at various business schools and corporate gatherings across the country.

Allison M. Paoli graduated from Saint Mary's College, Notre Dame with a B.A. in Communications and Advertising. Paoli also has an extensive background in the culinary arts. She attended Kendall College in Evanston, Illinois, the Scottsdale Culinary Institute, where she graduated with honors, and was awarded an apprenticeship at the prestigious L'etoile Restaurant on Martha's Vineyard. She currently works for Woodstone Consulting in Steamboat Springs, Colorado.

978-0-595-47118-8
0-595-47118-8

www.ingramcontent.com/pod-product-compliance
Lightning Source LLC
Chambersburg PA
CBHW030801180526
45163CB00003B/1117